Canada Under Attack

CANADA
UNDER ATTACK

Jennifer Crump

DUNDURN GROUP
TORONTO

Project Editor: Michael Carroll
Editor: Cheryl Hawley
Design: Courtney Horner
Printer: Marquis

Library and Archives Canada Cataloguing in Publication

Crump, Jennifer
        Canada under attack : Canadians at war / by Jennifer Crump.

Includes bibliographical references and index.
ISBN 978-1-55488-731-6

        1. Battles--Canada--History.
2. Canada--History, Military. I. Title.

FC226.C782 2010   j971   C2009-907481-8

1   2   3   4   5   14   13   12   11   10

 Conseil des Arts du Canada Canada Council for the Arts  Canadä ONTARIO ARTS COUNCIL CONSEIL DES ARTS DE L'ONTARIO

We acknowledge the support of the **Canada Council for the Arts** and the **Ontario Arts Council** for our publishing program. We also acknowledge the financial support of the **Government of Canada** through the **Canada Book Fund** and **The Association for the Export of Canadian Books**, and the **Government of Ontario** through the **Ontario Book Publishers Tax Credit program**, and the **Ontario Media Development Corporation**.

Printed and bound in Canada.
Printed on recycled paper.
www.dundurn.com

Dundurn Press
3 Church Street, Suite 500
Toronto, Ontario, Canada
M5E 1M2

Gazelle Book Services Limited
White Cross Mills
High Town, Lancaster, England
LA1 4XS

Dundurn Press
2250 Military Road
Tonawanda, NY
U.S.A. 14150

CONTENTS

To Alex, Laura, Emily, Alexandria, Kathleen, and Danielle.
For everything you do.

INTRODUCTION

In a December 2005 article in the *Washington Post*, journalist Peter Carlson concluded that while, "invading Canada is an old American tradition ... Invading Canada successfully is not." Carlson made that observation while covering a story on the declassification of War Plan Red, a 1935 document outlining the most recent U.S. plans to invade Canada.

Carlson may have had a point. Canada has been the scene of many invasions throughout its history. Our rich natural resources, kilometres of coastline, diplomatic ties, and proximity to the United States have made us a tempting target for the Americans and for other countries. Britain, France, Germany, Spain, Japan, and even Canadians themselves have launched invasions.

Some of these wars have been waged as part of a much larger conflict; others have focused on more local concerns. Wars that started on the European continent have frequently spread to Canadian shores and several have been concluded on Canadian soil. The Seven Years War involved nearly every major power in Europe and has been referred to as the first "world war." Battles were fought in Europe, Africa, and Asia, and on Canadian soil when the French attacked St. John's and the British invaded Louisbourg and Quebec City.

Some invasions occurred as part of a larger North American crisis like the American Revolution. Others began as local squabbles that erupted into global incidents. The Nootka Crisis began as a battle over a small patch of coastline on Vancouver Island and brought Britain, Spain, Germany, the Netherlands, and France to the brink of war. The Nootka Crisis claimed few lives, the Aroostook War none, but other major invasions like the War of 1812 took thousands of lives. The Battle of the St. Lawrence lasted for three years, the invasion of James Bay just a few days.

As Carlson pointed out, those invasions share one common theme: few succeeded and none succeeded for long. Invading Canada has been a long-time tradition for many nations. Invading Canada successfully has not.

CHAPTER ONE:
THE BATTLES OF THE BAYS

For centuries the ships of numerous countries visited Canada's eastern shores to reap the riches they found there. They would sail back to their home ports with their holds full and purses fat with profit. Norse, Italian, Spanish, Portuguese, British, and French fishermen all plied the waters near present-day Newfoundland. Some of the more adventurous among them would venture deeper into Canada, exploring its rivers and great inland seas in the hunt for furs.

Inevitably, they would clash.

While the Norsemen quickly abandoned the eastern shores of Canada and the Italians, Spanish, and Portuguese never settled the area, the French and English were soon engaged in a race to control the lucrative fishery and fur trade. Their approaches were initially quite different. The French preferred to have the furs delivered to them at Montreal, while the English preferred to set up shop closer to where the furs were. In 1670, the Hudson's Bay Company was created and its founders established Fort Charles on Hudson Bay. As the company expanded, they built additional posts at the mouths of the Moose and Albany rivers on James Bay. During the winter the posts were abandoned as the traders returned to Britain with their ships full of furs of every description. The French sent their own expedition to the area and made a show of claiming the land in their king's name, but there were no Englishmen there to witness it and whatever Native witnesses were in the area probably found the ceremony perplexing rather than threatening. For the next 10 years, the French and English traders grew more competitive although there were no outward signs of aggression until 1682, when traders from Britain, France, and New England all tried to claim the same trading post. The French won the initial argument but were pushed out by the British two years later.

In 1686, the new governor of New France, Jacques René de Brisay Denonville, decided to avenge this challenge to French sovereignty and to once and for all put an end the English presence on what he considered to be French soil. When the French government refused to lend him naval support he decided to organize and fund his own audacious overland attack on the Hudson's Bay Company posts on James Bay. In March 1686, Chevalier Pierre de Troyes was chosen to lead the attack. De Troyes began to gather provisions and recruit troops; 100 men would eventually join the expedition. Among them was the infamous Pierre le Moyne D'Iberville and two of his equally famous brothers. D'Iberville was one of 12 children born to one of the wealthiest citizens of Montreal, Charles le Moyne. Like his brothers, Pierre was a career soldier and a dedicated adventurer.

The le Moyne Legacy

Charles le Moyne de Longueuil et de Châteauguay, was an adventurer, businessman, and considered the wealthiest man in Canada during his lifetime. His 12 children, the le Moyne brothers, would become the most famous sons of early Canada. They found fame in the military as thorns in the sides of both the English and the Spanish, in politics as governors, and as the founders of several of the earliest settlements in North America. With an intriguing mix of personal ambition, respect for Native peoples, and intense loyalty to French Canada, they left a lasting legacy.

Following his successes in Hudson Bay and Newfoundland, Pierre le Moyne continued his adventures by founding Louisiana and the city of Biloxi, Mississippi. His eldest brother, Charles, achieved both military and political fame, receiving the title of baron and the successive governorships of Three Rivers and Montreal. Another brother, Jacques, was a respected warrior who whetted his military appetite by accompanying Pierre on his missions, subsequently gaining the respect of the French regulars, militia, and especially their Native allies. In 1689 he led a tiny force of less than 200 men in a successful attack on a British force of more than 1,300 on the banks of the Saint-Charles River. Jacques and his men routed the British but he was mortally wounded in the fight. When word of his death reached the Iroquois they released two captives in his honour.

Pierre's younger brother Paul accompanied him to Hudson Bay, famously leading a mission in which he captured a large English ship with only two small canoes. Paul also accompanied Jacques against the English invaders on the Saint-Charles River and helped defeat the Iroquois. He had spent many of his early years with the Iroquois and spoke their language fluently. Like several of his brothers, he developed a canny ability to undermine the English efforts to win the Iroquois over to their cause, alternately cajoling, bribing, and threatening during the councils of war he was regularly invited to join. Paul-Joseph, another brother, enjoyed an equally close relationship with Canada's Native peoples. He became governor of Detroit, Three Rivers, and Quebec City and rose rapidly in the military serving in France and Canada. At the age of 50, when many of his fellow officers retired, he was tasked with negotiating the terms of peace with the Iroquois, who considered him a blood bother. Another younger brother Jean-Baptiste founded Mobile, Alabama, and New Orleans, and served as governor of Louisiana, leading the French there against the Spanish and capturing the Spanish fort at Pensacola (Florida). Jean-Baptiste was one of the few le Moyne brothers to enjoy a peaceful retirement. Eventually recalled to France, he lived on generous pension granted to him by the king until the age of 88.

When the men prepared to strike out in the brittle cold of a Montreal spring day the excitement was palpable. In addition to a handful of regular soldiers, de Troyes had recruited 70 voyageurs, a hardened, independent group of fur traders known for their ability to survive under almost any conditions. Included in the expedition were two wealthy seigneurs and a priest, who watched as they began to assemble the sleds, canoes, and arms necessary for their journey. On March 30, the expedition set off on foot over the still frozen Lake of Two Mountains. Between them, the men carried their own heavy packs, guns, ammunition, and the eight 100 pound birch bark canoes they intended to use when the ice finally melted. The few sleds pulled by teams of oxen had been commandeered by the noblemen and the expedition's officers and were used to carry their luggage and personal effects. As they slowly made their way across the lake, the ice suddenly broke and a sled holding most of the Seigneur St. Germain's luggage almost plunged into the lake. The men were barely able to rescue the oxen, several of which did fall through the ice. A frustrated de Troyes ordered all of the oxen be sent back. The next day it was the men themselves who continually broke through the ice. The progress of the entire expedition paused as their fellow travellers dropped to their bellies and inched along the ice to attempt a rescue. De Troyes was out in front, leading them onward toward the Ottawa River, using his sword to test the thickness of the ice. Conditions worsened when a spring storm found them, pounding the river with heavy rain and high winds, and turning the frozen waters into dangerous slush.

After a brief stay on an island, which did little to warm their bodies or their spirits, the tiny army pushed on. On April 9, an advance party rushed back with the news that the Long Sault Rapids were just ahead and the best option was to drag their canoes up the rapids through the waist deep, ice-choked water. Some of the men, including de Troyes and the priest, Father Sfivy, opted for a route that took them along the craggy shoreline. But that difficult path severely damaged several of the canoes. They continued their assault on the rapids over the next five days. By then the undisciplined, rambunctious voyageurs had had enough. A fight broke out, fuelled by alcohol and exhaustion. One of the men had his jaw broken with the butt of a rifle. Once the officers had broken up the fight and settled the men, de Troyes called out the worst offenders, took their "eau de vie" away, and made them carry a sack of corn in its place. De Troyes, a career soldier, frequently despaired at his men's lack of discipline. By the end of the journey he would have even more to despair.

In the days following the fight, several voyageurs decided to help themselves to a cache of moose skins that had been hidden by one of the Native tribes that frequented the area. When the men returned with their loot, de Troyes promptly forced them to put it back. On April 14, Father Sfivy held high mass. Afterwards de Troyes divided the men into three brigades, providing each brigade with separate marching orders. He also implemented nightly guard duty in the hopes of instilling some semblance of discipline in the men, "which alone," he lamented, "is lacking in the natural worth of Canadians."[1] Discipline would remain a problem but de Troyes was nothing if not creative in dealing with problems. One unfortunate soul was tied to a tree for the duration of an encampment. Desertion also became a problem as the men suffered through the horrifying conditions. One by one they disappeared into the dense bush, never to be seen again. On April 30, four men deserted, taking one of the now precious canoes with them.

After that, progress was depressingly slow. Occasionally the men found themselves neck deep in water, their canoes held high over their heads, as they attempted to drag themselves through the rapids. Disgusted, a few of the voyageurs attempted to pole their way up the rapids only to wreck their canoes. On some days they managed to cover just eight kilometres in over 12 hours of travel. The rough conditions, boredom, and cold frequently caused serious illness and accidents. Burns were common. One man chopped a finger off while attempting to collect firewood. A keg of gunpowder exploded as the men celebrated May Day. Fortunately, no one was killed or injured. At the end of May the entire invasion almost came to an abrupt end when a forest fire, touched off by a campfire, roared down a hill toward them during a portage.

In May the force arrived at Lake Abitibi. De Troyes called a halt in order to build a replica of an English fort so that his men could practise capturing it. By June 8 he deemed the men ready to move on. But two days later one of his best soldiers, a man who had come the entire distance without being able to swim, drowned when the canoe he was travelling in tipped over while running a rapid. D'Iberville — who was travelling in the same canoe — survived, but lost most of his possessions. By then they were very near Moose Fort, de Troyes' first objective. There was barely time to bury the soldier and no time to mourn him. De Troyes immediately sent D'Iberville and several others ahead to scout the fort. Finally, at dawn on June 21, they attacked.

— — — —

Archives of Ontario

Moose Factory Fort.

England and France were not at war and relations with the local Natives were mutually profitable; the English had no reason to suspect an attack might be imminent. The 17 inhabitants of Moose Fort were still asleep when the French attacked, but they quickly rallied.

D'Iberville raced ahead of his men and made it through the gate just before the English managed to swing it closed. He was left stranded inside while his men outside tried to break down the gate and come to his rescue. D'Iberville managed to hold off the English soldiers for several long minutes before his men finally breached the fort. Within half an hour the English fur traders had surrendered, some still in their nightshirts.

Three days later, the French attacked Fort Charles. The *Craven*, a Hudson's Bay Company ship, was moored on the bay, just outside the fort. De Troyes dispatched D'Iberville and a handful of men to take the ship while he and the

CANADA UNDER ATTACK

remaining men surrounded the fort.

D'Iberville and his men rowed over to the ship and stole onto it, quickly overpowering the unsuspecting sailors on board. On the shore, de Troyes easily took the fort and commandeered D'Iberville's newly conquered ship to hold the loot he had gathered from the conquered forts.

On July 9, de Troyes attempted to return to Moose Fort, but became lost in the fog and did not find his way back for another week.

De Troyes then set his sights on Fort Albany. While the French bombarded the fort with canon borrowed from Moose Fort, D'Iberville witnessed a terrified woman running right into the path of an explosion. He and Father Sfivy dashed forward and, candle in hand, went from room to room looking for her. They finally found her, badly injured, lying on the floor in one of the rooms. D'Iberville reportedly carried her to a couch and called for a surgeon, then stayed with her while she was tended to, refusing entry to everyone else.

By the end of August, de Troyes was ready to return to Quebec. After naming D'Iberville as governor of the forts and assigning him 40 men to hold them, de Troyes headed back to Quebec to celebrate his victories. D'Iberville and his men survived the winter of 1686 before returning to Quebec in the summer of 1687, when no supplies arrived for their relief.

The forts that de Troyes and D'Iberville had worked so hard to secure were not to remain in French hands for long. By 1693, the British had retaken Fort Albany and the Hudson's Bay Company re-established the other forts by 1713.

After a brief return to France, D'Iberville returned to James Bay in the summer of 1688. As D'Iberville busied himself filling his holds with furs he was unaware that the English were planning to retake Fort Albany. As D'Iberville's ship tried to sail out of the mouth of the Albany River into James Bay, two English ships arrived to blockade him. The standoff lasted throughout the winter — while the English and French stared one another down the temperature dropped and all three ships became trapped in the ice.

D'Iberville was equally capable of compassion, honour, and unspeakable cruelty. It was his cruelty that won him infamy during his confrontation with the

CANADA UNDER ATTACK

English on the Albany River. When the English requested a truce in order to hunt for fresh game he denied them. Because they lacked adequate supplies the English crew starting showing signs of scurvy. When D'Iberville heard that the English were falling ill he sent word that he would allow the English surgeon to hunt. When the unfortunate surgeon ventured out, D'Iberville promptly arrested him. Although no shots were exchanged, several of the English died of scurvy, cold, and other diseases. Eventually the English were forced to surrender. D'Iberville took his ship back to Quebec full of furs and English prisoners.

For the next 10 years the English and the French would jockey for position in Hudson and James Bays, with first one and then the other seizing control. More often than not, D'Iberville was at the forefront of the French efforts. But he was seldom able to hold onto what he took and 10 years of warring in Canada's frozen north had wearied him.

D'Iberville was ready for a new challenge. He found it on the Atlantic coast, where the French and English were engaged in a battle for control of both the fur trade and rich stocks of fish. For more than a century, English and French fishing boats had operated in the waters off Newfoundland. Various settlements were founded by both countries, but they were isolated, sparsely populated outposts. They had little to do with one another and rarely came into contact, let along conflict, with one another. The populations of these outposts were extremely hardy people who had little experience with war. There were a few soldiers garrisoned in the far reaches of Newfoundland, but there did not seem to be much reason for them to be there. However, by the middle of the 17th century the English had greatly increased their presence in the waters southeast of Newfoundland. The area became known as the English Shores.

The French fishermen were unimpressed. Renewed interest in the fur trade, privateers who preyed on boats from both countries and rivalries from a far-off continent aggravated the tension between the colonies. The French heard that the English fishermen were making a fortune selling their salted cod to Spain and Portugal. They also knew that the English settlements, like Ferryland on the southern shore of the Avalon Peninsula, were isolated, sparse, and lacked basic defensive works. They would make easy targets. France called upon D'Iberville, fresh from his successes at Fort Henry, to drive the English from the shores of Newfoundland once and for all.

The French government wanted to have sole control of the region and gave D'Iberville the task of eliminating the English presence there. For his first target he chose Fort William Henry, along the Acadia-Maine border, close to present-day Bristol, Maine. The fort was easily taken and D'Iberville moved north. He arrived in the French capital of Placentia, Newfoundland, at the end of August 1696. In Placentia, D'Iberville clashed with the governor, Jacques-François de Monbeton de Brouillan, who, as the civilian representative of the Government of France, had ultimate command over the mission. De Brouillan had a reputation as a strong governor who had successfully defended his colony from repeated English attacks, but he was also a rapacious man who maintained a monopoly over trade and was rumoured to have forced his soldiers to take up fishing and then demanded a share of their profits. The Canadians and the Natives made things difficult for De Brouillan, refusing to follow anyone but D'Iberville, who, annoyed and frustrated by the conflict with De Brouillan, was threatening to return to France.[2] As a compromise, and likely to keep the two conflicting parties separated, France settled on a two-pronged attack led separately by both men. It was agreed that the governor would invade St. John's by sea and D'Iberville would take the more difficult land route to attack Ferryland. On November 1, D'Iberville and his men began to walk across frozen Placentia Bay. Nine days later, two of which were spent without provisions, they reached Ferryland. The journey was an arduous one; the Abbé Jean Baudoin recorded that, "We have walked nine days, sometimes in woods so thick that you could hardly get through, sometimes in a mossy country by rivers and lakes, often enough up to your belt in water."[3]

D'Iberville arrived at Ferryland to find that De Brouillan had already been there. His ships had set up a continual bombardment until the settlers begged for a truce,

[S]even sail of French ships of war and two fire ships landed about seven hundred men in Ferryland and attacked us on every side and after what resistance we could make against them (they being too many in number and too strong for us) we were forced to submit. And, for as much as we, your Majesty's most obedient and faithful subjects and petitioners, refused to take an oath of fidelity to the French king and take up arms against your most gracious Majesty, the said enemy dealt very hardly with us, and burnt all our houses, household goods, fish, oil, train vats, stages, boats, nets, and all our fishing craft to the value of twelve thousand pounds sterling [£12,000] and above and sent us away with our wives, children and servants, which are in number about 150 persons, who (through the mercy of God) are all safe arrived in this kingdom, although by reason of our said great loss reduced to great poverty and not able to subsist with our families without relief. [4]

By the time D'Iberville arrived, the village was virtually abandoned; all of the able-bodied men had gone to Bay Bulls to rebuild a fort there in anticipation of the French invasion. All who remained were those unable to travel: women, children, and old men, and they were all terrified. They believed that D'Iberville's men were capable of all kinds of savagery and they expected the worst. One woman reportedly threw herself into the sea when she saw the French approach.[5] The English settlers had every reason to be terrified. Over the next few months D'Iberville's conquest of the English coast would rival that of some of the world's most infamous and savage conquerors.

De Brouillan and his ships had already left to shell communities farther up the coast. Within days of arriving at Ferryland, D'Iberville and his men set out on the three hour march to Bay Bulls. The settlement offered scant resistance but a few days later D'Iberville's troops were ambushed by a small group of settlers just outside of Petty Harbour. Although they were poorly armed and lacked military leadership or training, the settlers held the French off for more than an hour. Before it was over, the English had lost nearly half of their men. After securing the prisoners, D'Iberville continued his march overland to Petty Harbour. After a brief skirmish, it too fell to the French. While these battles raged, a steady stream of terrified refugees had poured into St. John's, the English capital. Although lightly armed and without adequate provisions, they refused to surrender. D'Iberville was unperturbed and decided to provide the citizens with a little more incentive to give up the battle. "Seeing the inhabitants were about to defend themselves," wrote Baudoin, "we sent to Bay Boulle for the mortars and bombs and powder. On the night of the 29th and 30th MM. de Mins and de Montigny went with sixty Canadians to burn the houses near the fort."[6]

For three days, the citizens remained locked within the city walls, defying the French attackers. Then the French captured a hapless colonist by the name of William Drew. Holding him down, they ripped his scalp from his forehead to the nape of his neck and then sent it into the English fort with a warning that they would do the same to every Englishman there if they did not soon surrender.

This had the effect that D'Iberville was looking for,

> The 30th, the day of St. Andrew, a man came from the fort with a white flag, to speak of surrender. Afterwards the Governor with four of the principal citizens came for an interview. They would not allow us to enter the fort, lest we should see the miserable plight to which they were reduced. It was agreed they should surrender on condition of being allowed to depart for England. The capitulation was brought in writing to the fort, and approved of by the principal citizens and signed by the Governor and M. de Brouillon. [7]

Once the city had offered terms, D'Iberville quickly burnt it to the ground. As he had promised, he did send the citizens back to Britain but he forced all 224 men, women, and children to crowd onto a single tiny ship. The crossing, made in the dead of winter, must have been horrific for those aboard. Most would never return to Newfoundland. If they had, they would have found that the large, sophisticated settlement they had once called home had been completely destroyed. The English capital on the great rock was no more. It seemed to be the end of English rule on the Atlantic seaboard. Indeed, as the British Board of Trade informed their king, William III, the French were masters of the entire island.

Master or not, D'Iberville was not yet finished. His orders had been to drive every Englishman from Newfoundland, and he was determined to do so. He dispatched small raiding parties to wreak terror across the remaining outposts of the English colony. No hamlet or cove — no matter how tiny and insignificant — was spared. His men burned, looted, and took prisoners, expelling every English man, woman, and child they encountered. In just four short months, D'Iberville destroyed 36 settlements. Only two managed to defy him: Bonavista and Carbonear Island. Of the latter, Baudoin wrote,

> Around 9am we also left in five shallops for Carbonear. Passing in front of the point of the island of Carbonear, we saw the enemy lined up in great numbers. They fired a few canon shots at us. On this island were the people of Carbonear, of Harbour Grace, of Mosquito Cove, of other little harbours, and the refugees from St. John's. They seem to be about 200 men, already lodged in barracks which they have made since they started worrying we would come … We cannot attack unless we are insane, unless we have more than 200 men. "The abbé continued, somewhat ominously," Besides which, there are still many other places to take.[8]

But tiny Carbonear proved to be D'Iberville's undoing. When he left for France, still unable to take the island, the English Navy finally arrived, spurred to action by the report given to them by the English Board of Trade. New English forts were constructed and a significant military presence was permanently garrisoned on the island. By the spring of 1697, 1,500 British troops were guarding the island. The settlers were slowly enticed to return and in less than 12 years the population of the island exceeded what it had been when D'Iberville invaded.

Archives of Ontario

Forts on Hudson Bay. By that time, D'Iberville's attention had return to Canada's northern bays. He made one last, spectacular attempt to invade the James Bay coast, heading north on a perilous journey at the head of a flotilla of French ships. A deep fog settled on the Hudson Straight and D'Iberville's ship, the *Pélican*, became separated from the rest of the fleet. He found himself surrounded by three English warships. D'Iberville knew that it was imperative that he prevent any English ships from reinforcing the English forts in the bay, so rather than attempting to flee the ponderous English vessels, he fired upon them. In the resulting firefight, D'Iberville managed to sink one of the English vessels and capture a second, which sank soon after. The third ship fled. By then the *Pélican* was also sinking from damage caused by the English ships. D'Iberville managed to unload his ship just before it sank and just as the other ships from the French fleet arrived. Over the next few days the French and English engaged in several lively battles, but in the end the English governor surrendered to D'Iberville. As D'Iberville

CANADA UNDER ATTACK

sailed out of the Bay for the last time, leaving it confidently in the hands of the French, a treaty was already being hammered out by representatives from Britain and France in the Dutch town of Ryswick. The treaty ignored what D'Iberville had achieved, giving Fort Albany and Hudson Bay to the British and the lower James Bay to the French.

CHAPTER TWO:
LOUISBOURG UNDER SIEGE

The French and English were still battling for supremacy on the east coast almost 50 years later. The French had Louisbourg but the English had their New Englanders. The latter were just as determined to remove the French presence from the Atlantic coast as D'Iberville had once been to remove the English.

On the cloudy, moonless night of May 10, 1744, the English found their opportunity. Darkness had fallen early and as it did a motley collection of fishing boats, bateaux, and small merchant ships slipped their moorings outside of Canso, Nova Scotia. On board were a ragtag collection of would-be soldiers: students, clerks, and farm boys seeking adventure; and adventurers seeking booty. Few of the men had any military experience and though there were cannons on board, there were no trained gunners to man them. Fuelled by rivalry, revenge, and religion, the men headed toward Louisbourg, Nova Scotia, to capture the fortress and force the French Catholics out of the colonies.

Many people, including most of the colonists who had volunteered, considered the invasion a fool's errand. The fort was widely considered to be impenetrable. In a letter to his brother, the venerable Ben Franklin urged caution and warned that, "fortified towns are hard nuts to crack; and your teeth are not been accustomed to it … But some seem to think forts are easy taken as snuff." [1]

Louisbourg was the Gibraltar of the West, an impenetrable bastion designed with the lofty goal of ensuring the survival of the French Empire in the Americas. The Treaty of Utrecht had stripped French North America bare. They had been forced to give up most of their prized possessions: Acadia, Rupert's Land, and Newfoundland. All that remained were Île-Saint Jean (Prince Edward Island) and Île Royale (Cape Breton Island), a tiny island of rock and bog upon which France's future in North America would rest. Upon that rock they began construction of a massive fortress, the largest and most indestructible in North America. They called the fortress Louisbourg, after their king.

The fortress stood guard over the St. Lawrence and controlled access to France's inland possessions, including Quebec City. The fortress also protected the French fishing boats that vied with the English for access to valuable fish stocks, and the numerous French privateers who preyed on vulnerable English colonial merchant ships. Unfortunately, Louisbourg served as a beacon, a constant reminder to the New Englanders and other English colonials of the French presence in North America. They viewed its creation with increasing irritation and a growing conviction that their duty to Britain lay in the destruction of Louisbourg, and of the French influence in North America.

It would not be an easy task. The fortress had cost the French treasury over 30 million livres[2] to build and its upkeep and repair were a constant strain, but by 1745 it loomed menacingly over the gateway to the St. Lawrence. Lying in front of the fortress was a deep harbour, protected on the south side by reefs and an island battery that functioned more like an independent fort. Only three boats could land at the single, small beach, and most of the time the surf prevented even that. To the northwest the French built another battery, the Royal Battery, with twin swivel guns mounted in its towers that could swing between the harbour and the fort. Twenty-eight more 42-pound guns were aimed directly at the harbour entrance. Larger ships were forced to enter the bay via a narrow, 152-metre wide channel, between the Island and Royal Batteries and under the watchful eyes of the battery gunners. At the edge of the island, Canada's first lighthouse provided direction along the craggy shore to the hundreds of boats that visited the fort every year. There were natural protections as well: the swells outside the harbour were unpredictable and the area was notable for the thick, impenetrable fogs that frequently blanketed the landscape.

The fortress itself was impressive. Outer walls that were 1.5 metres thick stretched for almost five kilometres around the site, enclosing just over 100 acres. The fortress walls were nearly 11 metres thick and nine metres high. There were places for 148 cannon and a 25 metre wide moat encircled the entire fort. The defences to the rear of the fort were less intimidating, but the French engineers who built it were not anticipating a land invasion. Besides, several kilometres of thick swamp stretched across the land beyond the fort, swamp the engineers considered to be impassable.

The site was near perfect for defence.

The New Englanders watched as the fort grew in size and influence. They also saw the ships leaving the busy harbour of Louisburg bound for France, their holds filled with valuable cargoes of dried, salted cod, and returning loaded with wine, foodstuffs, and finery. By 1744, they felt they had seen enough. They began to make plans to invade and force the French Canadians from the shores of North America for good. One of the most ardent lobbyists for the invasion was Governor William Shirley of Massachusetts. Like many governors of the period, he was also a merchant and felt the losses inflicted by competing French merchants and French privateers.

There had been whisperings of an invasion for months. American merchants and politicians were lobbying hard, trying to convince the British and colonial governments to support their efforts to evict the French. But before any invasion could take place, the War of the Austrian Succession began, pitting France against Great Britain once more. By stroke of luck, the French Canadians received word of the war a full three weeks before their New England counterparts. They saw this as their opportunity to restore French North America to its former glory.

The French soldiers attacked a small New England fishing fort at Canso, captured it, and took several captives back to Louisbourg. Then they turned their attention to Annapolis Royal, Nova Scotia, with the intention of liberating Acadia from the British. But the French were outmanned and outgunned and the Acadians showed little enthusiasm for the cause. After a half-hearted attack, the French withdrew back to Louisburg.

The New Englanders were still hesitant to attack Louisburg. A secret ballot held in both the senate and the legislature denied the governor the power to launch an invasion. The fortress, their experts argued, was too strong, too impenetrable; the invasion of Canso was regrettable, but in the end it was not worth a war. But the Puritan public, already irritated by the close and competing presence of French speaking papists, forced another vote and finally the invasion was approved. Governor Shirley wrote to his neighbours requesting their support. Massachusetts sent over 3,000 men, New Hampshire and Connecticut sent 500 each.

The force gathered at Canso and waited impatiently for the ice to thaw. While they waited the officers attempted to drill their men, and preachers shouted outdoor sermons lauding the soldier's courage and the justness of the mission. Sometimes the cacophony made it difficult to distinguish between preacher and officer. As one diarist put it, "Severall sorts of Busnesses [sic] was a-Going on: Sum a-Exercising, Sum a-Hearing o' the Preaching."[3]

By the time the New Englanders began to gather at Canso, Louisburg was already eroding from within. Because they were caught up in battles closer to home, France had failed to adequately supply or repair the fort. In December, the small force of regular soldiers at the fort, a mere 560 men, mutinied after discovering that government officials were cheating them out of their rations. The mutiny was diffused, but the cheating continued and government and military officials regarded each other with growing resentment. The only other defenders were the militia, which comprised the largest part of Louisburg's fighting force and included nearly every Cape Bretoner who could stand and hold a musket. There were young boys and old men, nearly 1,300 in all.

Despite the clear rumblings that warned of an imminent invasion, little was being done within the fort to prepare. Councils of war were called and there was a lot of discussion, but no action was taken. Instead, they waited for reinforcements. France had promised an additional 2,000 troops to launch a full-scale invasion of Acadia. Rumours of the imminent arrival of a Quebec guerrilla fighter named Marin, along with a small force of First Nation and Quebec fighters, buoyed the residents of Louisbourg. It could only be a matter of time before the French soldiers arrived. Unfortunately for Louisbourg, neither Marin nor the promised French reinforcements arrived.

Within the walls of the fort, life continued in much the same way it always had. The civilian population, which easily equalled that of the military, continued to work, trade, and live their lives. Their confidence returned as the threat of invasion seemed to fade. The fortress was, after all, impenetrable.

A few worried voices did reach out to France, chiefly that of an anonymous inhabitant of Louisbourg who warned of the imminent invasion and the ill-equipped fort that would attempt to repel it. The warning went unheeded. The expected reinforcements from France failed to arrive and the New Englanders launched their attack. Luck, wrote the habitant, was clearly on the side of the New Englanders. Even the weather co-operated. "The English … seemed to have enlisted heaven in their interests," he wrote. "So long as the expedition lasted, they enjoyed the most beautiful weather in the world."[4] The wild winds that usually whipped the Cape Breton coastline abated, the fog that enshrouded it lifted. On the morning of March 14, the habitant watched in horror as host of British American ships entered the bay, coming from all directions: Acadia, Boston, Placentia…. The invasion had begun.

Although the habitant, locked securely in the fortress of Louisbourg, could not have known it, two French ships did eventually try to come to the rescue of Louisbourg. The first, the *Renommée,* had been sent in January and was forced to wait until the ice had broken up before it could reach the area. Finally, at the end of March it sailed by Canso, where it caught the attention of the English who pursued the ship until its captain finally gave up and returned to France. A second French ship, the *Vigilant* was dispatched loaded with provisions and carrying a full contingent of reinforcements, some 600 men. The *Vigilant* sailed into Louisbourg harbour on May 20 and again the British gave chase. A fierce battle raged through the day and night, and finally the French ship struck its colours. No more reinforcements would be sent; Louisbourg was on its own.

On board one of the English ships was a merchant named William Pepperell, who had been handpicked by Governor Shirley to lead the expedition. Pepperell, like most of the Massachusetts militia, had no military experience, but he was well respected, sensible, and committed to the cause. The mission itself had begun to take on almost a crusade-like atmosphere as religious leaders in the colonies whipped up anti-Catholic and anti-French fervour. One of the chief advocates of these sentiments was the evangelical leader George Whitfield. But despite his zealous support for the cause in his pulpit, Whitfield had warned his friend Pepperell that he would be envied if he succeeded and abused if he failed.[5] Both men believed the latter was the far likelier outcome.

Carefully hiding any misgivings he may have had, Pepperell sailed his flotilla into Gabarus Bay, alongside four ships commanded by the British Commodore Peter Warren. Almost immediately the bells of Louisbourg began to peel out a warning and a canon fired a single shot. Citizens from the surrounding countryside scurried to safety behind the fortress' great walls. Also inside, the anonymous habitant decried the ill-conceived French raid on Canso. "The English would perhaps not have troubled us if we had not first affronted them,"[6] he wrote. The habitant appeared to have an intimate knowledge of the fortress and had reservations about its ability to withstand an assault. In his letter he refers to several unrepaired breaches in the walls of the Royal Battery. In his official report the acting governor of Louisbourg admitted that many outer defences had been destroyed in advance of a longer term plan to rebuild them.[7]

Unfortunately for Louisbourg, Governor Shirley was also very familiar with the fortress's flaws. The prisoners taken at Canso had returned from Louisbourg with a detailed description of the fort, and the information they lacked was supplied by the many merchants who had carried on an illicit and very profitable trade with the fort for years. Shirley gathered this information and drafted a complex plan of attack for Pepperell to follow. The plan was an interesting one. It called for Pepperell to make his landing at night. Once on land, the force would separate into four parts. The first two would advance toward the walls in complete silence. The third would approach the Royal Battery and also wait in complete silence for a prearranged signal. The final silent group would approach the fort from the beach, climb the walls, and capture the governor. Shirley expected all of that to be accomplished undetected and in unfamiliar territory.

Pepperell might have lacked military experience but he certainly recognized a ludicrous military plan when he heard one. After a quick feint that drew the

French in another direction, he landed his troops several kilometres to the southwest of the fort in the daylight, setup camp, and dispatched troops to do some reconnaissance. The troops raided nearby farms and then discovered and set fire to the naval storehouses. Then their commander, William Vaughn, made camp for the night, allowing his men to scatter and find their own way back. By morning there were only 13 men remaining. Rather than risk running into a French advance force, he decided to return to Pepperell and the main camp. On their way they passed to the rear of the Royal Battery. No smoke rose from fires, no guards walked the rampart, only silence called to them from behind the high walls. Vaughn and his 13 soldiers crept closer, but there was still no sign of life from within the battery. They bribed a local Mi'kmaq who, feigning drunkenness, stumbled up to the gate of the fort. He found the entire battery deserted. The French soldiers, shaken by the fires and the blinding smoke of the burning naval storehouses, had slipped away in the night.

Vaughn marched his small band of men into the fort and one of the youngest shimmied up the flag pole, tore down the French blue, and replaced it with his own red jacket. Vaughn then penned a quick letter to Pepperell requesting a proper flag and few additional men to hold the battery. They also discovered that the French had made a fateful mistake in their hasty abandoning of the Royal Battery. They had failed to spike the guns or destroy the stores, leaving the invaders with easy access to arms and munitions, both of which they immediately turned on Louisbourg with devastating effect. Within the fortress walls, the booming guns of the Royal Battery wreaked havoc as houses collapsed and the inhabitants ran in terror into the streets.

Pepperell then set his sights on Louisbourg itself. Within sight of his encampment lay the perfect venue from which to launch an attack on the fortress city: the high hills that surrounded its walls. But between Pepperell and the hills lay exposure to Louisbourg's formidable guns and a deep, murky bog that stretched for several kilometres. The first attempt made by the army to cross it ended disastrously with the colonists' guns lost in the thick mud. Finally, one of the soldiers designed a gun-sleigh that could be pulled across the marsh. Up to

200 men manned each sleigh, making slow, painful progress across the wet bog. Orders from their superiors had them travelling only at night or under cover of one of Louisbourg's notorious fogs. Experience eventually taught them to take a different route every time, since crossing the bog twice in the same location turned the ground into an impassable soup. Each morning, as the sun rose over the ocean, the soldiers, wet, cold, and exhausted, would take refuge behind a boulder or tree and try to sleep as the French shells landed all around them. Then, as darkness fell, they would pick up their ropes and continue their trek toward the hills.

Pirates and Privateers

Pirate attacks were a frequent, and occasionally fatal, annoyance during the War of 1812. In fact, Canadian pirates, sanctioned by local governments and the British navy, helped win the battle for the Atlantic coast, capturing dozens of American ships and winning a fortune in prizes for their owners.

But the War of 1812 was not the only time that pirates sailed Canadian waters. Eighteenth century French privateers regularly harried the Massachusetts coast from their home port at Fort Louisbourg. These pirates were also a key participant in the defence of Port Royal and Louisbourg from the English who would have taken it. Canadian privateers were also active throughout the Napoleonic Wars. When the French disrupted Nova Scotia's profitable trade with the West Indies, Canadian pirates retaliated by attacking French and Spanish merchant ships. That venture proved even more profitable than the original trade with the West Indies had been. The Rover was the most infamous of the Canadian pirate ships of that time. It quickly established a reputation as a ship with a crew as ruthless and they were undefeatable, even against incredible odds. Working alone, the crew of the Rover once attacked a convoy of seven merchant ships, seizing three of them; in another instance it engaged three Spanish warships and defeated all of them.

With its numerous isolated settlements and expansive coastline, Canada was also a favourite hunting ground for pirates from other nations, particularly in the

CANADA UNDER ATTACK

earliest days. One of the first pirate attacks occurred in 1582 when a pair of English pirates raided Portuguese and Spanish fishermen on the Avalon Peninsula. In 1668, Dutch privateers twice raided the Avalon, burning ships, houses, and chattel in the harbour and briefly taking St. John's. But when they returned in 1673 the people of St. Johns were ready for them. They laid a heavy chain across the harbour that caught and held the Dutch ships. Before they could disengage themselves, the men of St. John's sent a small flotilla of fire ships toward the Dutch pirates, burning several of them to the waterline and forcing the rest back out into the Atlantic.

By May 4, the colonials had set up a battery on Green Hill, less than 1,500 metres from Louisbourg. They had also managed to turn several of the guns from the abandoned Royal Battery back onto Louisbourg. The soldiers continued to roll the guns toward the hills, setting up batteries and not slowing until they set up their final advance battery less than 225 metres from the west gate of Louisbourg. It seemed, at least for a few moments, that Louisbourg might collapse easily and quickly. Within Louisbourg itself, the prospects seemed bleak. Soldiers and citizens alike took refuge when the shelling was at its most intense and crept out during the occasionally lightening of the barrage to repair the damage. It was a futile task. The shells fell almost continuously and building after building was destroyed. By the time siege ended just one house remained standing.[8] Provisions were scarce. For days no one had ventured from the fortress and no relief ships had found their way in. No reinforcements arrived from Annapolis or France. The men, women, and children of Louisbourg were on their own. Food was scarce and strictly rationed with the choices bits saved for the officers and government officials. From outside the walls they heard the taunts of the British soldiers only metres from their front gate. The defiant return taunts of their own soldiers did little to buoy their spirits. No action was taken; no soldiers marched to meet the enemy. There were rumours that the French governor had received a demand for surrender from the English and that he had turned it down, there were countless councils of war but nothing seemed to happen. Instead, they waited, hungry, exhausted, and terrified. Whether they waited for reinforcements or rescue no one was really certain. The only thing they could be sure of was that the colonists waited outside their doorstep and on nearly every hill surrounding the city that was crumbling around them.

There was a solution, but the French commanders did not seem to see it. The colonial flanks were clearly exposed and unprotected. The French just had to send out troops to attack the isolated batteries, but the commanders feared the tenuous hold they had on their men after the recent mutiny. The habitant lamented that the commanders did not dare send out their troops to challenge the English for fear that the unhappy, recent mutineers might join the enemy.[9]

The New Englanders had problems of their own. The eager, inexperienced gunners would frequently overload their canons, causing fatal explosions. Insubordination was also rampant, as was drunkenness. The men frequently ignored orders and alcohol inhibited their ability to fight and occasionally resulted in their not showing up to the fight at all.

Warren and the British Navy hovered just outside the harbour, held back by the guns of the Island Battery. They were eager to join the fight and Warren constantly pressed Pepperell to take action against the battery. But while the colonials were able to secure the lighthouse, the battery remained defiant. The first four plans to attack were abandoned. On the first actual try, most of the 800 colonial soldiers came to the battle drunk and the officer in charge of the operation failed to show up at all. In a second attempt, the colonials crept up to the battery under cover of the area's notorious fog. Once one third of the men had reached the beach undetected, a few inebriated soldiers called out three cheers for their success. The French immediately opened fire and for the next several hours, chaos reigned. When the smoke and fog finally cleared, over 60 colonials lay dead and several hundred had been taken prisoner. The Island Battery still belonged to the French.

Warren still pressed to join the fight and Pepperell knew that success in Louisbourg depended upon his capture of the Island Battery. A second attempt was merely a matter of time and careful planning. Pepperell salvaged a number of heavy guns that had been sunk by the French just beyond the lighthouse and ordered his men to construct a battery near the lighthouse to house them. The lighthouse offered an unmistakeable advantage — its elevation was much higher than that of the Island Battery and, once completed, the salvaged guns could be pointed directly into the small fort. They completed work on the fort on June 10, and almost immediately opened fire on the Island Battery. For two days they kept up a steady barrage that ended with many of the French fleeing into the surf and taking their chances swimming to the fortress. By nightfall on the twelfth, the Island Battery was in colonial hands. Almost immediately the British sailed into the harbour eager to join the fight.

The citizens of Louisbourg had seen enough. Their soldiers were exhausted, as was their supply of gunpowder. Within days the Circular Battery had been reduced to ruins and the west wall completely destroyed. The colonials were in control of the West Battery itself and had turned its terrifying guns down into the city they had been designed to protect. The British were massing their fleet in front of the city. The citizens petitioned the government to end the siege. After 45 days of relentless shelling, the siege was finally lifted. The acting governor, Duchambon, initiated a surrender in which the French would be allowed to march out in their colours and the citizens within Louisbourg would be granted safe passage to France along with all of their property.

The colonial soldiers, many of whom had joined in hopes of reward, were angry that the loot they had hoped for would be denied to them. They would be angrier still when they finally realized the consequences of "the Greatest conquest, that Ever was Gain'd by New England."[10] But in the meantime, cities in both the colonies and Great Britain celebrated the victory over Louisbourg with speeches, picnics, and fireworks. In London, the Tower guns were set off and more fireworks illuminated the skies. Warren, Pepperell, and Governor Shirley all gained tremendous rewards and accolades. Warren was made a rear admiral, Pepperell received a baronetcy, and Shirley received the lucrative right to raise regiments. But not everyone found their riches in the invasion. William Vaughn, the erstwhile captain who had so buoyed the invasion with his taking of the Royal Battery, travelled to London hoping for reward. He received no recognition and instead contracted smallpox and died in the winter of 1746. The rest of the men received no riches and only the momentary gratitude of their fellow New Englanders. Two thousand of them also received notice that they were expected to continue their occupation of Louisbourg until they could be relieved by a force on its way from Gibraltar. The force failed to arrive. Pepperell wrote to his wife,

> We have not as yet any answer to our express's from England, and it being uncertain whether I shall return this winter, although it is the earnest desire of my soul to be with you and my dear family, I desire to be made willing to submit to him that rules and governs all things well; as to leave this place without liberty. I don't think I can on any account.[11]

Conditions within the fort were nothing short of brutal. The men lived in squalid, filthy conditions in the ruins of the fort. The sickness that had plagued the troops over the cool, wet summer worsened as the weather got colder. Once winter had closed the fort off from any new provisions or relief the sickness worsened. Between November and January, 561 English soldiers were buried at Louisbourg, many beneath the floorboards when the ground became too frozen for the survivors to dig graves.[12] That number is staggering compared to the total loss of 130 men during the siege: 100 to gunfire and another 30 to disease. By February, Pepperell commanded just 1,000 able-bodied men; the other 1,000 had been felled by sickness or death. The British governor wrote of his time in Louisbourg, "I have struggled hard to weather the winter, which I've done thank God, tho was not above three times out of my room for five months … I am convinced I shou'd not live out another winter in Louisbourg."[13] To further compound their troubles, the men received minimal pay and found their protests falling on deaf ears. In one dramatic episode, a group of New Englanders marched to the parade ground without their officers and tossed their weapons down. A British Navy officer, who had witnessed both the conditions at Louisbourg and the protest, remarked that he had always thought the New England men to be cowards but he thought that if they had a pickaxe and a spade they would dig their way to hell and storm it.[14]

In March the promised relief finally arrived and the surviving colonists were allowed to return to their families. A small group of them took a souvenir with them: a large iron cross from the cathedral at Louisbourg. Eventually finding its way to Harvard, the Louisbourg Cross remained at the university for nearly 250 years until they finally agreed to permanently loan it to Canada in 1995.

But in 1746 the battle was still going on, at least in the eyes of the French. On the heels of the British reinforcements a flotilla of French warships had also headed toward Gabarus Bay, intent on retaking the fort and redressing the humiliations suffered at Louisbourg. But luck and weather once again favoured the English colonists. The French fleet was plagued by illness, beset by storms, and harried by the English Navy until it finally gave up and abandoned its mission to retake Louisbourg. The English who were in command of the fort were elated, but their joy soon turned to disgust when news reached them that during the negotiations of the Treaty of Aix-la-Chapelle the British had traded Louisbourg back to the French in return for the small fort of Madras in India. Everything the colonists had fought for had been abandoned; the French commanded the mighty fort of Louisbourg once more.

The French were not able to enjoy the fort for long. By 1757 they were back at war with the British, and both the Americans and the British had once again set their sights on Louisbourg. They started slow; first isolating Louisbourg by confining the first fleet of reinforcements sent to the city and then by defeating a second fleet sent out to rescue the first. A third fleet finally made its way to the island but its commander, worried about a possible invasion, decided to lead his ships to the relative safety of Quebec. His concerns were justified. The French had made some important improvements to the fortress. They were no longer exposed along the swampy east; instead they were protected by lines of guns and trenches, fronted by a further defence called an *abatis*, felled trees that were sharpened and pointed towards the advancing enemy. Despite the French having strengthened the fortress it was still a tempting target because it controlled access to Quebec and the rest of French Canada.

With Quebec City as the final target, the British planned two major campaigns. The first, involving over 15,000 men, was launched against Fort Ticonderoga on

Lake Champlain, while Major-General Jeffrey Amherst led a 12,000 man force toward Louisbourg. Among the officers that Amherst selected to launch the attack on Louisbourg was a young James Wolfe, who would go on to lead the invasion of Quebec City and end French hegemony in North America forever. While the British locked down all of the ports from Nova Scotia to South Carolina, in order to keep the invasion secret, Amherst gathered his troops in the newly built Fort George in Halifax. Within weeks they were joined by nearly 14,000 sailors and marines. Within Louisbourg, a force of barely 7,500, and 4,000 civilians, waited nervously for the inevitable invasion.[15]

As dawn broke on June 1, 1758, the shocked Louisbourg sentries finally spotted the first sails of the massive invasion force anchored in Gabarus Bay. Rough seas kept them at anchor but the swells calmed and in the early hours of June 8 the entire fleet doused their lights while 2,000 soldiers slipped into the small bateaux that would carry them to shore. They bobbed in the water, waiting for the signal that would launch a three-pronged attack on three French beaches. At 4:00 a.m., the ships began to fire on Louisbourg and the fortress answered with the steady beat of drums sounding the *générale* — the call to arms. Most of the French forces turned a steady, terrifying barrage against the tiny boats. Several boats overturned and the soldiers, weighted down by their heavy uniforms and packs, sank to the bottom of the bay. As a horrified solider looked on, "One boat in which were Twenty Grenadiers and an officer was stove, and Every one Drowned."[16] Standing at the bow of his boat, his red cape flapping in the wind, General Wolfe made a tempting target. But the French held their fire until the boats were well within musket range, and then let loose a furious barrage that left Wolfe desperately waving the accompanying boats back with his cane. They attempted to turn around amidst heavy fire from the French and rough waves that pushed them back toward the shore.

It seemed that the massive invasion, so carefully planned, was going to end in unmitigated disaster. But then, as occasionally happens in war, fate intervened and saved the day for the British and colonials. Officers aboard three of the boats spied a rocky outcropping beyond the range of the French guns and turned toward it.

C.W. JEFFERYS

Wolfe Walking Ashore Through the Surf at Louisbourg.

Wolfe immediately ordered the ships nearest him to follow and they pulled their boats onto shore beyond the view of the French. The French Governor Augustin de Boschenry de Drucour was stunned to learn that the British and Americans had made land. Instead of launching a counterattack, he elected to pull back. He ordered the Royal Battery destroyed and abandoned. A day later he ordered the Lighthouse Battery destroyed and then withdrew his men into the fortress.

Wolfe barely missed a beat. He marched his almost 2,000 strong army around the bay with an eye to taking and rebuilding both the Lighthouse and Royal Batteries so that they could be used against Louisbourg. In the meantime, Amherst kept his own army busy building a road through the sand, bog, and marsh in preparation for an attack by land. In a replay of the 1745 attack, hundreds of men were put to work pulling the massive guns into position. On June 18, the soldiers were startled to hear the sounds of a naval battle occurring within Gabarus Bay. They did not know it then, but de Drucour had attempted to smuggle his wife and several other women out of Louisbourg to the safety of Quebec. Madame de Drucour and her companions were taken from the defeated French ship and returned with honour and consideration to her husband at Louisbourg. Despite the courtesy of the British, for the remainder of the siege Madame de Drucour climbed the fortress ramparts daily to fire three canon shots in honour of the king of France. Amherst was so impressed with the lady's courage that he sent her a letter and a gift of two pineapples with several messages and letters from captured Frenchmen. Another flag of truce appeared and a basket of wine was delivered to Amherst with the compliments of the governor and his wife. As soon as the wine was delivered the canons roared to life on both sides. Courtesy and compliments aside, there was still a war to be won.

The defence of Louisbourg must have seemed hopeless even to the most optimistic of the French troops. But de Drucour refused to surrender, knowing that the longer he held out the less likely it was that the British fleet would move on to Quebec. By the end of June the walls of Louisbourg were crumbling and the city had no defences beyond what was left of them. Then, a British bomb exploded in the magazine on board one of the French ships. As the magazine

The Expedition Against Cape Breton in Nova Scotia, 1745.

exploded, sparking a horrific fire, the British continued to pound the ship with cannons and the fire spread to two nearby ships. French soldiers and sailors leapt into the sea, exchanging a fiery death for a watery grave.

Five days later the British launched a sneak attack at midnight on two of the last remaining French ships, the *Prudent* and *Bienfaisant.* They slipped aboard, released the English prisoners held on the ships and then set fire to the ship's magazines. Once the French realized what was happening they immediately fired back at the English ships. Within hours, the *Prudent* was in flames and the *Bienfaisant* had been sunk.

To those inside the fortress it must have seemed like the British and Americans were everywhere. Their canons dominated the hills around the city, their ships clogged the bay, British soldiers had taken up key positions in trenches along the perimeter of the city, and a steady barrage of canon fire had wreaked havoc on the city. The British lines had moved up so close that their front lines could pick off the French soldiers one by one on the ramparts above the city. One habitant wrote,

> Not a house in the whole place but has felt the force of their cannonade. Between yesterday morning and seven o'clock to-night from a thousand to twelve hundred shells have fallen inside the town, while at least forty cannon have been firing incessantly as well. The surgeons have to run at many a cry of '*Ware Shell!*' for fear lest they should share the patients' fate.[17]

Finally de Drucour agreed to sue for peace. The terms were exceedingly humiliating for the French troops, but without them the safety of the civilians could not be ensured. Drucour had to content himself with the knowledge that he had prevented an attack on Quebec City; it was far too late for the British to continue their attack, at least that year. So the French surrendered and de Drucour was shipped as a prisoner to Britain. Louisbourg was once more in British and American hands. The British continued in their attempts to rid the Atlantic coast of French settlements and in 1759 would use Louisbourg as a launching point for an attack on Quebec. That invasion would be Louisbourg's last. In the 1760s the fort was razed by British soldiers who did not want to see it returned to the French in any future peace treaty.[18]

CHAPTER THREE:
THE BATTLE OF QUEBEC

With Louisbourg in English hands, the seemingly endless war for control of North America appeared to have shifted in favour of Britain. The next battle would decide the war and pit two of the greatest generals that North America would ever know against one another. Their chosen battleground would be another fortress city: the city of Quebec.

Quebec was the cornerstone of New France and the lynchpin in the machine that ensured French hegemony in the region. It was there that European ships went to trade and where the furs were sent to be shipped to Europe and elsewhere. From Quebec, adventurers, traders, and soldiers had access to ports extending into the Great Lakes and the fur-rich interior of Canada, and outward to the Atlantic and the ports of Europe. Militarily, the city appeared impenetrable. It was situated on a very narrow portion of the St. Lawrence where the shores stood barely one kilometre apart. The Saint-Charles River curled into the St. Lawrence there, providing a natural haven for ships in the Beauport Bay. The city had been built atop an unassailable series of cliffs, which formed a natural fortress-like barrier between the city and any potential bombardment from the river below. The city itself was divided into two parts: Upper Town and Lower Town. Lower Town contained the piers, shops, and homes of many of the common people and was situated on a plain along the banks of the river. Upper Town was home to the clergy and upper classes, and was located on a high cliff that ran parallel to the river. A thick battery with two heavily fortified gates separated the two parts of the city.

To land their fatal blow, the British chose James Wolfe, a temperamental career soldier who had honed his craft at the brutal Battle of Culloden. At the age of 13 he received his first post as an officer in his majesty's navy and soon developed a reputation as a brilliant tactician, somewhat unorthodox soldier, and a man destined for great things. After Louisbourg fell, largely because of Wolfe's fearless efforts, he lobbied hard for the invasion to be carried on into Quebec. He wrote to his superior, General Amherst:

> [W]e might make an offensive and a destructive war in the Bay of Fundy and in the Gulf of St. Lawrence. I beg pardon for this freedom, but I cannot look coolly upon the bloody inroads of those hell-hounds the Canadians; and if nothing further is to be done, I must desire leave to quit the army.[1]

When Amherst and others refused to move on Quebec as quickly as he would have liked, Wolfe returned to England. Despite being a man plagued by various illnesses, he chafed at inaction. In London he lobbied for another promotion and an assignment to lead an invasion of the fortress of Quebec. Wolfe's exploits at Louisbourg had captured the imagination of the British public, who had heard nothing of the brutality with which he crushed any resistance from the inhabitants of the Bay of Fundy and the Gaspé. But not everyone was enthused with the idea of Wolfe's potential as a leader. When it was suggested that he be given command of the Quebec campaign, a story circulated that Wolfe's superiors considered him mad. "Mad is he?" King George is said to have replied. "Then I hope he bites my other generals."[2]

Wolfe frequently wrote about the imperfections of his character and considered himself quick-tempered and even cruel. "My temper is much too warm," he wrote in a letter to his mother, "and sudden resentment forces out expressions and even actions that are neither justifiable nor excusable."[3] Yet he had an unflappable loyalty to his country and an immoveable sense of justice and honour. When a superior officer ordered him to shoot a wounded highlander at Culloden he refused, risking his own ambitions, a court martial, and possible hanging rather than violate his own sense of honour. But this same sense of justice would later lead him to condone acts of horrendous violence against citizens who supported the French.

In February 1759, Wolfe sailed with the British fleet across the Atlantic; with him were some of the nearly 9,000 troops who would form his invasion force. Others awaited him in Louisbourg. Nearly one third of his force came from the American colonies, many of them German and Swiss settlers with a considerable number of American backwoodsmen and sharpshooters thrown into the mix. Among the remaining two-thirds were an entertaining mix of British regulars, highlanders, and Irish. Many of the Irish were cast-offs from the regular army, pardoned convicts, and pressed men. The traditionally dressed highlanders included a regiment known to the French as *les sauvages sans culottes*, a group known particularly for their ferociousness in battle. Regulars were drawn from regiments previously assigned to battlefronts on the European continent and included three regiments from the soldiers assigned to guard Louisbourg during the winter of 1746. Of the latter group, one of Wolfe's officers wrote, "They made a very shabby appearance and did not trouble themselves much about discipline; nor were they regularly clothed; their officers seemed to be a good deal ashamed."[4] Wolfe was blunter, believing "that no good could be made of them"[5] But whatever their faults, Wolfe's army consisted of the toughest, most experienced and battle hardened troops ever to launch an invasion in Canada.

The trip across the Atlantic proved slow and rough, particularly for Wolfe, who was prone to seasickness. He arrived in Louisbourg, ill and ill-tempered, and furious to discover that none of the ordered preparations for his invasion had been accomplished. Ice had apparently delayed the small fleet of ships that was to have sailed up the St. Lawrence in advance of the main fleet to capture incoming French ships and prevent reinforcements and supplies from reaching Quebec. Though the ice had prevented the British ships from sailing it had not, Wolfe quickly learned, prevented the French ships from reaching Quebec. When Wolfe arrived in Louisbourg, prepared to launch an immediate invasion, he learned that not only were the French aware of the coming attack, but they had already received both the provisions and the men they would need to withstand a lengthy siege. The hungry, desperate rabble he hoped to face were well-fed and well armed.

Within Quebec City itself, the mood was generally buoyant. Despite the news that the British were on their way, provisions and reinforcements had arrived. Surely the mighty fortress of Quebec could withstand the assault. But one man feared that the battle might be the last to be fought on French North American soil. Like Wolfe, Louis-Joseph de Montcalm-Gozon, Marquis de Montcalm, was a career soldier. He became an officer at 12 and was wounded no less than five times during a career that led him to French battlefields all over the world. By 1759 he was nearly 50 years old, anxious to resume his retirement, and a reluctant commander of the French forces in the New World. In a letter written in April 1759, Montcalm informed the war minister in France that he fully expected Quebec to fall, if not that year then surely the next.[6] The response from the French government was clear. A letter from the minister of war informed Montcalm that it was,

> [N]ecessary that you limit your plans of defense to the most essential points and those most closely connected, so that … each part may be within reach of support and succor from the rest. How small soever may be the space you are able to hold, it is indispensable to keep a footing in North America; for if we lose the country entirely, its recovery will be almost impossible.

Despite the reluctance with which he accepted his assignment, Montcalm was an honourable and loyal soldier, determined to protect the colony. He pleaded in vain for both substantial reinforcements from France and a shoring up of existing defences within Canada. Both pleas had fallen on deaf ears. France was too consumed by the war on the continent to spare much for its far-off colony. In Canada Montcalm had to negotiate with the colony's corrupt business manager, Françoise Bigot, and the inept French Governor François-Pierre de Rigaud de Vaudreuil. Bigot's job was to preserve stores for the colony but his business was in commandeering all the local crops and sending them to France on government ships. Governor de Rigaud would then inform the government that the colony was starving and Bigot's friends would sell the crops back to the government at a rich profit, to ship back to the very colony they had been stolen from.

For his part, Governor de Rigaud was less concerned with the defence of the colony than he was with his own amusement. He was convinced that the rumoured British invasion force would be unable to navigate the treacherous St. Lawrence and would be wrecked on one of its numerous shoals. When Montcalm suggested defending Pointe-Lévy, across the river from Quebec, de Rigaud's engineers scoffed that no known gun could land shells on Quebec from that great a distance. Both of those assumptions would prove to be fatal mistakes.

Montcalm was in Montreal when the French ships slipped through the English net and made their way up the St. Lawrence. Montcalm hated Montreal at least as much as he detested Quebec. He was appalled by the drinking and gambling that the nobility, especially de Rigaud and Bigot, indulged in. The excesses seemed even more decrepit to him when, during the long winter of 1758–1759, the soldiers were put on half-rations and forced, on some occasions, to eat their horses while the local peasantry, dependent upon stores from France for sustenance, simply starved. The endless parties, dinner parties, and balls wore on Montcalm and he longed to be in the thick of battle or at least preparing for battle again. Then the ships from France arrived. While he welcomed the reinforcements and supplies, what really buoyed his spirits were the letters from France conferring upon him sole responsibility for the defence of Quebec and stripping both de Rigaud and Bigot of much of their power. Montcalm hurried to Quebec, making the journey in little over a day. He quickly launched a massive project to build batteries and earthworks, but years of neglect made the job challenging. Montcalm considered the effort critical and, unlike de Rigaud, he was not content to allow the volatile St. Lawrence to take care of the English fleet for him.

The English fleet was not about to trust the St. Lawrence either. For much of the winter of 1758–1759, two British officers — Samuel Johannes Holland and James Cook[7] — had been busy charting the Gulf of St. Lawrence and the St. Lawrence River. They painstakingly measured the river's depth by carefully tossing in a weighted rope, allowing it to slip through their hands until the weight rested on the bottom, and carefully noted every sandbar, pool, and inlet. Guided by Holland and Cook's charts, Wolfe's army was ferried uneventfully up the St. Lawrence by a naval fleet commanded by Admiral Charles Saunders in early June 1759. What the charts could not help them with was the treacherous traverse just downriver from Quebec. Saunders's second in command, Rear-Admiral Philip Durell, travelled ahead of the others and made his way through by subterfuge. Drawing near the traverse, he raised the French colours and several pilots canoed out to help him steer through. Once the pilots were captured, he lowered the French colours, raised the British, and forced the pilots to lead his ships through the dangerous rapids. On board, Saunders had an unfortunate French captain who was forced to choose between loyalty to his country and his life. He chose the latter and the entire fleet slipped easily through the traverse. The fleet was an imposing sight. It stretched for kilometres along the St. Lawrence and included 50 warships, a score of frigates, brigs, and sloops, and 119 transport and supply ships.[8] The sight of this massive English fleet must have terrorized the French Canadian peasants who watched its arrival. But if this sight shocked them, the English were equally shocked by what they found on the French shores.

Wolfe had initially decided to make his landing at Beauport, between Quebec and Montmorency Falls. But when the ships arrived just outside Beauport they found a heavily fortified encampment of batteries and large guns that stretched for almost 10 kilometres along the coast. Behind the fortifications lay the French troops, a good number of the 14,000 to 16,000[9] that Montcalm had at his disposal. Wolfe was not disturbed by the comparative strength of the French Army; he considered them nothing more than "five feeble French battalions mixed with undisciplined peasants."[10] But he did recognize that an assault by water against such a heavily defended location as Beauport would be suicidal. He met with his three most senior officers — Robert Monckton, James Murray, and George Townsend — to consider his options. There were not many. Wolfe had centred most of his plans on enticing Montcalm out to attack him. He expected that battle to be a furious one but he also expected to win it. Unfortunately for the British, the French refused to come out from behind the safety of their battlements. After a brief, ineffectual resistance from the handful of French troops stationed on the island, Wolfe landed most of his army on the Île d'Orléans and set up camp there.

A few days later he dispatched rangers to explore the terrain and entreat the locals to stay neutral in the conflict to come. Those who resisted were taken prisoner, but he treated the women and children with respect and promptly returned them to the French. In fact, he invited one group of captured gentlewomen to dine in his tent, exchanging pleasantries with them and inquiring when Monsieur le Marquis might be convinced to come out and fight him. One of wittier of the ladies responded with a quote from Plutarch, "If thou art a great general, Marius, come down and fight." She paused and then continued her quote, "If thou art a great general, Silo, make me come down and fight." There is no record of Wolfe's response but it was clear that he wanted nothing more than for Montcalm to come down and fight. Such pleasantries quickly came to an end when de Rigaud claimed that Wolfe only returned the prisoners because he had no food to feed them. All prisoner releases were immediately halted. Wolfe continued to believe that the Canadians would prefer to remain neutral, but to ensure that he had proclamations nailed to the doors of churches in villages all over the region. The proclamations included the usual posturing regarding the inevitable outcome of the conflict. But they also warned that, "should you suffer yourselves to be deluded by an imaginary prospect of our want of success; should you refuse these terms, and persist in opposition," he would be ruthless in crushing them. "If by a vain obstinacy and misguided valour, they presume to appear in arms, they must expect the most fatal consequences their habitations destroyed, their sacred temples exposed to an exasperated soldiery, their harvest utterly ruined, and the only passage for relief stopped up by a most formidable fleet."[11]

On the night of June 28th, as all but the sentries whom Wolfe had appointed lay sleeping in the British encampment at Île d'Orléans, a small group of French ships made their way toward the British fleet at anchor outside the island. As the French ships drew near they suddenly burst into flames. They were fire ships, their sole purpose was to sail into the enemy's craft and destroy them. The French had

The Defeat of the French Fireships attacking the British Fleet at Anchor before Quebec, 28 June 1759.

spent considerable time and money on this strategy. Bigot had himself sold the fire ships to the French government, at a considerable profit of course.

The fireworks were magnificent, but not very successful. One of the French captains had lost his nerve and fired his ship too early, followed by five of the other captains. Only one had held out — Captain Dubois de la Milletière. De la Milletière kept his ship on course, hoping to reach the British fleet, but the other ships soon lit his ablaze and the captain and his valiant crew were killed in the conflagration. The general alarm was sounded on the island and one of the British ships nearest the fire ships cut its cables and drifted farther down river, out of reach of the flames. No real damage was done. Smaller British craft towed the flaming ships out to the middle of the river where they burned harmlessly to the waterline.

While the rangers were scouting the Quebec countryside and the invaders waited impatiently, and increasingly nervously, on Île d'Orléans, General Robert Monckton led a few additional troops to the undefended Pointe Lévy, where they set up a battery across from Quebec. The soldiers in the Lower City of Quebec lobbed jeers and insults across the water at the British. Their engineers had, after all, assured them that no shells could reach the town from the headland across the river. The first shell launched by the British landed in the water and the jeers grew louder. The next shell landed in Upper Town and the jeers abruptly stopped. The British kept up a relentless bombardment for the next two months, laying waste to much of the city. Curé Richér recorded in his journal that over 40,000 cannonballs and 10,000 firebombs fell on his city during those two devastating months.[12] Sister Marie de la Visitation was working in the city's convent hospital when the barrage began. The British were armed she wrote, "with all the artillery that the infernal regions could supply for the destruction of mankind."[13] As the bombardment continued, Sister Marie recorded the devastation and terror inflicted by the British. "The only rest we partook of," she wrote, "was during prayers, and still it was not without interruption form the noise of shells and shot, dreading every moment they would be directed towards us... During one night, upwards of fifty of the best houses in the Lower Town were destroyed."[14]

But artillery and explosions were not the only plagues that faced Quebec City's inhabitants. Famine was a constant threat, as was sickness brought to the colony by the French reinforcements and exacerbated by shortages of food and medicine. Sister Marie de la Visitation's own small convent was forced to feed some 600 refugees. Scores of other residents fled the city for the relative safety of the countryside, but the danger followed them.

By the end of July, Wolfe had grown tired of the endless wait. Montcalm still wisely refused to come out to fight him. The siege was dragging on and soon winter would set in and Wolfe would be forced to either abandon the attack or allow his ships to become trapped in the ice and force his army to take their chances surviving as best they could the formidable Canadian winter.

Drawing of Quebec City.

Wolfe had discovered that although they may not have loved the French, the Canadians were willing to help them defend their territory. Rangers turned up dead, one with a stake driven through his heart. English foraging parties were attacked and killed, and occasionally sentries were found pinned to their posts with tomahawks. Wolfe penned another proclamation and when it too was ignored, he dispatched raiding parties to burn crops and villages, and take prisoners in an effort to terrorize the populace into submission. By then, Wolfe, plagued by stomach upsets and symptoms of scurvy, was too ill to leave his bed. Many of his men believed him to be dying.

The "King" of Newfoundland

David Kirke was a merchant and adventurer, an interesting hybrid born in Dieppe, France, but with strong economic ties to England. Early in the 17th century, at the height of the Thirty Years War, David Kirke's father and several other London merchants established a trading company to sponsor trade and settlement along the St. Lawrence River. Expelling their French rivals from North America became one of the company's, and therefore the Kirke family's, raison d'être.

In 1628, David Kirke sailed from London in the company of his four brothers and almost immediately captured Tadoussac, a small French trading post near Quebec. With an almost regal bravado, Kirke sent a party of Basque fishermen to Champlain to demand that he surrender Quebec to England and the Kirke's. Expecting the imminent arrive of supply ships, Champlain declined and Kirke decided not to attack the fortified city. While leading his ships back across the Atlantic, Kirke encountered the French supply fleet and easily captured them, putting the Quebec colony, still dependent on support from France, in a very precarious position. In France, David and his brothers, considered to be traitors in their country of birth, were burned in effigy.

But the English were very impressed with the success of the Kirkes and offered them sole rights to trade and settle in Canada. In 1629, David Kirke returned to Quebec to find the colony near starvation and Champlain much more willing to offer terms. He accepted Champlain's surrender of the colony in July 1629. David was knighted for his services to the crown and in 1637, after Quebec was returned to the French in the treaty that ended the Thirty Years War, he was given co-proprietorship of Newfoundland and settled in Ferryland. There he lived like royalty and controlled most of the economic activity on the island. He ousted those in control, collected taxes, established taverns to serve the fishermen, and strictly controlled fishing rights around the island. When the Puritans took control of England he hired his own 400 strong navy of "fishermen" to guard against a possible attack. Like any self-appointed king, Kirke had his detractors and was eventually brought up on state charges that he had withheld tax monies from the crown while a private suit was launched against his for his purported "seizure" of the Province of Avalon. No charge was ever substantiated but Kirke died in prison before he was exonerated.

Montcalm steadfastly kept to his plan. The fire ships had failed but the weather was growing steadily colder. If the coming winter did not drive the English away, it would most certainly kill them. While he waited, he reinforced the road to Montreal and kept his inexperienced troops inside the fortifications. The bombardment of the city troubled him but he did not dare risk his untested men in an attempt to take Pointe Lévy. When a group of merchants came to him to beg to be allowed to attempt to retake the Pointe he refused. Eventually he relented and a small militia led by the merchants launched a counterattack on Pointe Lévy. In the dead of night on July 11, 1,200 militia, fortified by 200 Jesuit divinity students and a handful of regulars and Natives, rowed across the river to a beach several kilometres west of the British battery. In the dark woods, the militia became separated into confused, armed mobs and at least three times fired upon each other. Despite hearing that the British remained unaware of their position and listening to pleas from their commander to stay the course, nervousness turned to panic and they fled back to their boats and across the St. Lawrence.

The incident further reinforced Montcalm's determination to wait out the enemy, but his soldiers were less convinced. Worried about their families, they began to desert. De Rigaud made another attempt to scatter the English flotilla with fire ships. This time he sent 70 ships and the commander waited until they were nearly in the midst of the British fleet before setting them ablaze. But again, the British seamen rowed out and towed the ships into the river. An angry Wolfe sent a message to the French warning that, "If you presume to send down any more fire-rafts, they shall be made fast to the two transports in which the Canadian prisoners are confined in order that they may perish by your own base invention."[15]

The summer dragged on and still Wolfe was unable to come up with a comprehensive plan to take Quebec. On July 31, in a desperate bid to end the siege, Wolfe ordered his troops to make a disastrous attack near Montmorency. Just as the French began to run out of ammunition the weather broke. The raging storm that followed gave the advantage to the French. The British were forced to make their advance up a hill that was much steeper than Wolfe had anticipated and was covered in deep mud, all while the French were firing down upon them. The English quickly retreated and the attack was soon abandoned. Nearly 1,000 British troops were killed during that battle and another skirmish that took place when an advance party was sent out to locate a ford near Montmorency. Due to rampant illness, poor sanitation, and the summer heat another 2,000 troops were sick or dying. Wolfe was finding himself increasingly at odds with his officers. Everyone was anxious. Leaving would be a failure on the grandest scale, one that would threaten the careers of everyone involved. Still, Wolfe could not come up with a plan that would neither be suicidal nor ineffectual. In a letter to his mother he lamented his predicament,

> My antagonist hast wisely shut himself up in inaccessible entrenchments, so that I can't get at him without spilling a torrent of blood, and that perhaps to little purpose. The Marquis de Montcalm is at the head of a great number of bad soldiers and I am at the head of a small number of good ones, that wish for nothing so much as to fight him; but the wary old fellow avoids an action doubtful of the behaviour of his army.[16]

Wolfe rose from his bed to pitch a plan of attack; his junior officers immediately dismissed it and, dejected, he returned to his bed. The officers devised a plan of their own that called for an invasion 64 kilometres upriver and would allow the British to cut-off French supply lines. They hoped that would finally draw Montcalm into a battle. Wolfe initially agreed to the plan, which called for the troops to land near Pointe-aux-Trembles, but heavy rains first delayed then prevented the landing entirely. While the troops regrouped, Wolfe changed the plan. He had spied another potential location for a landing: the cliffs at Anse-au-Foulon. It was, in many ways, a much riskier plan than the one proposed by his officers. For one thing, there were massive cliffs that the armies would be forced to climb before they could make the battlefield. Another potential problem was that landing at Anse-au-Foulon would put the British troops between the two most heavily manned French positions. However, landing there would allow Wolfe to greatly enhance his numbers with easy access to the troops holding both Pointe-Lèvy and Île d'Orléans.

With little fanfare, the navy began to move Wolfe's troops upriver. At dusk on the evening of September 12, one of the British ships began to fire on the French troops at Bougainville, drawing French attention away from Anse-au-Foulon. Fortune was finally smiling on Wolfe. A French supply ship was expected and orders were given to do nothing to jeopardize its safe arrival in Quebec City. Although the supply ship never arrived, most of the French troops did not know and would follow their orders, exercising an abundance of caution in their dealings with the English in fear of harming their own supply ship. As darkness fell, Wolfe and his troops slipped into boats and schooners and silently began to row toward shore. A French sentry challenged the boats and a fast thinking officer quickly answered him in French. When they were challenged again, the same officer told them to shut up or "you'll give us away to the English." As his boat bumped up against the shoreline, Wolfe leapt onto the beach, the first man to do so, and quietly ordered the men behind him to take the path to the guard post at the top of the cliff. Luck intervened there as well. The officer in charge of the sentries had let many of his men return home to help with the harvest. The remainder were quickly overwhelmed by the English soldiers, except one who escaped to sound the warning.

Neither Montcalm nor de Rigaud believed the news when it was brought to them. The English could not possibly be launching an invasion now, and certainly not where the sentry claimed they had landed.

> As we came into la Canardière courtyard, a Canadian arrived from the post of Mr de Vergor, to whom the Anse-au-Foulon post had been entrusted truly at the worst of times. This Canadian told us with the validation of undisputed fear that he was the only one who had escaped and that the enemy was on top of the hills. We well knew about the difficulty of forcing our way through this place even when it was barely defended, so that we did not believe a word of the account of a man whose head, we thought, had been turned by fear.

CANADA UNDER ATTACK

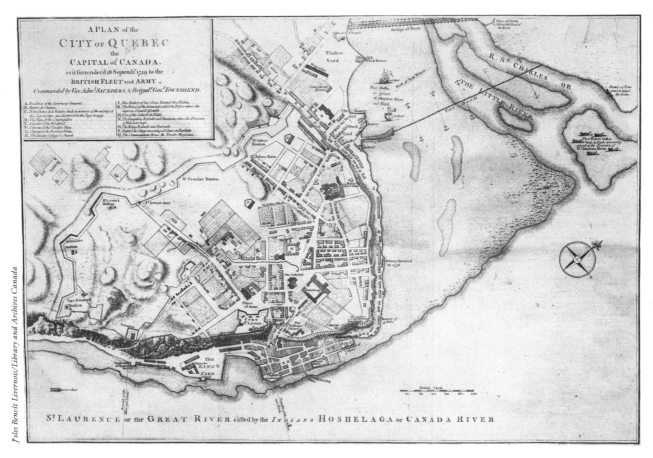

A sceptical Montcalm hurried to a vantage point overlooking the Plains of Abraham and saw hundreds of redcoats spilling over the edge of the cliffs and onto the flat, hard ground beyond the city.

As Wolfe massed his troops at the edge of the Plains of Abraham, and handfuls of rangers captured surrounding houses, Montcalm considered his options. He could wait for reinforcements to arrive from Bougainville. He had barely 3,000 troops on hand, and most of those were militia. He could not strip the city of its defenders, but on the other hand there did not appear to be too many British soldiers. He also could not afford to wait. As he explained, "We cannot avoid the

A Plan of Quebec City at the Time of the Siege, 1759.

issue. The enemy is entrenched; he already has two pieces of cannon. If we give him the time to establish himself, we'll never be able to attack him with the few troops we have. Is it possible that Bougainville doesn't know this?"[17] Unfortunately for Montcalm, the rough terrain hid many of the invaders. He made the call to advance immediately on the British. The difference between the two armies was never as obvious as it was on the Plains of Abraham. Montcalm's inexperienced militia ran forward in a disorganized charge, shooting wildly. Few of their bullets found their intended targets. Wolfe's experienced troops advanced slowly in a solid red line, holding their fire until they neared the French troops and then, in unison, they took careful aim and fired their weapons. The volley hit the French line like a devastating tidal wave. The French quickly broke ranks and began an equally disorganized retreat to the fort.

Wolfe was in the midst of his men, urging them on. One of the first volleys launched by the French caught him in the wrist. Another caught him in the stomach, but he forced himself forward. Almost at the same time, Montcalm was struck in his side by a British musket and he was carried from the field. Wolfe, mortally wounded, finally fell to the ground. An aide tried to ease his pain by telling him of the battle's progress. When the aide announced that the enemy was routed, Wolfe is said to have proclaimed, "[N]ow I can die in peace." He rolled over on his side and died shortly thereafter. Montcalm would die the next day of the injuries he had sustained early in the battle.

Within the city, other leaders met to discuss whether to defend or surrender. Montcalm's aides urged them to fight on. They had nearly 13,000 men, a force far larger than that commanded by the British. But the city fathers and many of the officers had lost their general; they were sick of war and far less confident in the unseasoned troops. They decided to sue for peace. The siege of Quebec was over.

CHAPTER FOUR:
THE FOURTEENTH COLONY

While Wolfe's career ended on the Plains of Abraham, the career of one of his most trusted lieutenants began there. Guy Carleton had been the officer to whom Wolfe entrusted construction of the British batteries. When war once more brewed on the continent, Carleton would be the man who the British government allowed to control defences for Quebec. Other than two tiny islands at the mouth of the St. Lawrence River, the French had abandoned the Canadian colonies. But the British and French were no longer the only ones interested in eastern Canada. For years the population of the 13 British colonies south of the St. Lawrence had separately brooded over taxation and attempts by the British to limit colonization of the North American west. In the spring of 1775, the brooding exploded into violent confrontation near the towns of Concord and Lexington. Those 13 colonies joined the battle to dislodge their British masters.

They had once hoped to be 14.

Quebec was just one of several colonies invited to join the Continental Congress in their fight against British tyranny in 1774, but it was considered the ideal prize. The hated Quebec Act had greatly enlarged Quebec's borders and the colony encased the entire Ohio Valley, among other choice territories. The Americans labelled the act one of the Intolerable Acts and called for its immediate revocation by the British. The territorial slights were bad enough but the Canadians were also denied *habeas corpus*, trial by jury, and representative government under the act. Surely, the Americans reasoned, despite the grants of land, the French Canadians were as outraged by that as they were. It did not occur to the Americans that the French Canadians would not embrace the idea of ridding themselves of the British yoke. The Quebec Act had also guaranteed the French Canadians language and religious freedoms. That alarmed the American leaders, though it must have reassured the Canadians.

The delegates to the Congress drafted a letter and had it translated into French. Two thousand copies were printed and delivered to Canada. In the open letter to the citizens of Quebec, distributed on October 26, 1774, the Americans urged the Canadians to join their cause and become the 14th colony.

> Seize the opportunity presented to you by Providence itself. You have been conquered into liberty, if you act as you ought. This work is not of man. You are a small people, compared to those who with open arms invite you into a fellowship. A moment's reflection should convince you which will be most for your interest and happiness, to have all the rest of North-America your unalterable friends, or your inveterate enemies. The injuries of Boston have roused and associated every colony, from Nova-Scotia to Georgia. Your province is the only link wanting, to compleat the bright and strong chain of union. Nature has joined your country to theirs. Do you join your political interests. For their own sakes, they never will desert or betray you. Be assured, that the happiness of a people inevitably depends on their liberty, and their spirit to assert it. The value and extent of the advantages tendered to you are immense.

The colonies' arguments seemed, to them at least, to be perfectly sound and logical. Quebec was joined to the American colonies by geography; it only made sense that the colonies forge political ties as well. To add more punch to their argument they pointed out that Quebec was much smaller and less populous than the rest of the colonies and therefore it would be in Quebeckers best interest to count the Americans as friends rather than enemies. What the Americans did not include in the letter was that they were equally perturbed by the clauses in the Act that ensured the preservation of the French language and gifted numerous rights to French Catholics and perks to the French Catholic clergy. A young Alexander Hamilton, who would later earn fame as one of the founding fathers of the United States, even penned a pamphlet in which he warned that another Inquisition was imminent and American heretics would soon be burning at the stake.

When their first letter was ignored, the Americans sent another on May 29, 1775. That time they entreated the Canadians to join the cause, arguing quite eloquently that they considered the Canadians friends and disliked the idea of being forced to consider them enemies.

In Canada, unsettled by events in the south, the British governor, Sir Guy Carleton, called up the local militia. But having lent two regiments of regulars to the defence of Boston, he had just 800 men at his disposal to protect all of Quebec. He needed the militia but no one wanted to join. The habitants were annoyed that the power to tithe had been restored to the Catholic Church and the Seigneuries, and they were not about to risk their lives to protect them. They were also tired of war and of their farms and fields serving as battlegrounds for foreign troops. Both the British and the Americans had drastically misjudged the Canadians. They were not willing to join the revolution but they were not interested in actively resisting it either. "We have nothing to fear from them while we are in a state of prosperity," Carleton wrote, "and nothing to hope for when in distress. I speak of the People at large; there are some among them who are guided by sentiments of honour, but the multitude are influenced by fears of gain, or fear of punishment."[1]

While Governor Carleton accepted that the French were allies of convenience only and could not be counted on to defend the country, the Americans refused to accept that the French would not eventually embrace their cause. Popular wisdom within Congress suggested that it was only a matter of time before the oppressed French joined with their American liberators. They just needed to be convinced that the Americans were serious. The way to do that, many suggested, was to invade the country. Once the Americans were at their door, the French would embrace them. Canada, George Washington firmly believed, was ripe for the taking. A young colonel by the name of Benedict Arnold was dispatched to open up the lightly defended route to Lake Champlain. He struck first at Ticonderoga (Fort

Benedict Arnold, American general, traitor, and would-be conqueror of Canada.

Carillon), where they met a brief challenge from the single sentry and then roused the commander of the fort from his sleep so he could surrender. Less than 50 men defended Ticonderoga.

Crown Point, the next fort in their path, was even more lightly defended: nine British soldiers guarded the fort. They wisely offered the Americans terms. Buoyed by his quick successes, Arnold ventured over the border to attack Fort St.-Jean. Lacking sufficient troops to hold the fort, he satisfied himself by burning a British ship and helping himself to some of the British stores.

The road to Canada was wide open. Congress was finally ready to act and plans were laid for an invasion. It was to be a two-pronged attack. The first 2,000 man force would be lead by General Philip Schuyler and would use a route that would take the army across Lake Champlain and then up the Richelieu River to invade Montreal and then Quebec City. A second force of just over 1,500 men, commanded by Benedict Arnold, would launch from Boston and head directly to Quebec City.

Schuyler arrived at Ticonderoga in the middle of July and immediately began to train the inexperienced, undisciplined troops. By early September he finally felt they were ready and he led them along Lake Champlain to the tiny island of Île-aux-Noix in the Richelieu River. By the time the troops had arrived on the island, Schuyler was ill. Eventually he grew too ill to lead and ceded command to

CANADA UNDER ATTACK

Brigadier-General Richard Montgomery, who launched a series of quick raids into Canada. The focus of the raids was the British controlled fort of St.-Jean.

Fort St.-Jean had been on the alert since Arnold's raid in May. Governor Carleton had dispatched 140 regulars, accompanied by 50 members of the Montreal militia. Additional troops of Native warriors were assigned to patrol around the fort. As the sole guard on the road to Montreal, Fort St.-Jean was a critical element in controlling the colony; Carleton was as determined to protect it as Montgomery was to conquer it. The first attempt by Montgomery, on September 7, failed miserably. Quebec newspapers reported that a mere 60 Native warriors had driven off nearly 1,500 American soldiers. Worse news awaited the Americans. An American sympathizer living near Fort St.-Jean, Moses Haven, arrived with the news that while the habitants were sympathetic to their cause, they had no intention of joining the Americans until there was clear evidence they would be victorious.

Not all Canadians remained neutral. Mistreatment by the Americans encouraged some to actively support the British. Others, for various reasons, actively worked for the Americans. When war broke out, James Livingston, a resident of Montreal, recruited an army of men from Chambly, Quebec, to aid the Americans. He was eventually given commanded of that army, known as the First Canadian Regiment of the Continental Army.

Montgomery decided they might have better luck with a night attack. Two days later he led a 1,000 strong force back up the river. While Montgomery and several other officers waited by the boats, his men scattered into the woods that lay between the river and the fort. In the confusion of the dark woods the Americans began to fire on one another, and they made a hasty retreat back to boats. A furious Montgomery sent them back out again, but this time the Americans met a small party of Native warriors and habitants. Once again the troops retreated to the boats. As their commanders met to discuss a new strategy, rumours spread that a British warship was on its way. This sparked a mass panic and the Americans fled back to Île-aux-Noix, almost leaving their commanders behind.

Although their attempts to take the fort were unsuccessful the Americans surrounded it, essentially cutting it off from the rest of Quebec. The same sickness that had felled Schuyler, exacerbated by the damp swampy ground of the island, began infecting many of the American soldiers. To make matters worse, several days of stormy weather delayed the next attempt on Fort St.-Jean. The Americans had more luck on September 17, when they managed to capture a supply wagon headed toward the fort and drive back the Canadian militia that had ventured out to retrieve it.

Despite their efforts, the Americans could not draw out the main force and the Canadians refused to surrender. But with hundreds of women and children inside, and food supplies running low, it was only a matter of time. Fort Chambly, to the east of Fort St.-Jean, had fallen on September 20. Montgomery dispatched Ethan Allen's forces to guard the road to Montreal. Not content with simply enforcing the siege, Allen took his 250 men to the gates of Montreal. There they engaged with a smaller Canadian and Native force before breaking ranks and retreating back toward Fort St.-Jean. Carleton bolstered the troops and gathered 2,000 Canadian militiamen to defend Montreal. But when the siege dragged on and no orders were given to relieve them, the men drifted back to their homes and farms for the fall harvest. The Americans continued to tighten their hold and finally, on November 3, as an early fall snow storm set in, Fort St.-Jean capitulated.

The people of Montreal were already nervous. As General Montgomery approached, and forts and farms alike fell to his army, they grew terrified. Within the city chaos reigned as merchants and citizens raced to hide their valuables and pack their belongings. A few stopped to watch in horror as the garrison of soldiers scur-

Ethan Allen

Ethan Allen, a businessman, farmer, and experienced guerrilla leader, was best known as the leader of the Green Mountain Boys, a fiercely independent paramilitary militia that had formed in southern Vermont in the decade before the Revolutionary War. By 1775, Allen and his "boys" were lending their substantial military experience to the war effort, and the revolutionary government turned to them to help with the capture of Ticonderoga.

CANADA UNDER ATTACK

ried to pack their own belongings. Then the news filtered out that Carleton himself had slipped out of the city and was headed to Quebec City in a flotilla of tiny whale boats. Any hope of an attempt to defend the city was lost. The final blow came with a directive from Governor Carleton, who was safely ensconced within the walls of Quebec City. Montreal must be abandoned, he wrote.

On November 17, Carleton arrived in Quebec City where he learned that a second force was headed toward him from Boston. Montgomery arrived two weeks later and set up camp outside the city. Once again the two generals had a common objective. Both felt that the city of Quebec was the key to controlling Canada. Despite the fact that his troops controlled every other major fort within Quebec and had overrun most of the colony, Montgomery refused to claim victory. "I need not tell you," he wrote, "till Quebeck is taken, Canada is unconquered."[2] While Carleton believed that Quebec would be his last stand against the American invasion and that holding the city was crucial, he was less convinced that he would be successful. He mistrusted the citizenry. "Could the people in the town be depended upon," Carleton wrote to Lord Dartmouth. "I should flatter myself, we might hold out.... But, we have as many enemies within, and a foolish people, dupes to those traitors, with the natural fears of men unused to war, I think our fate extremely doubtful, to say nothing worse."[3]

His distrust of the populace led Carleton to issue a proclamation shortly after his arrival in Quebec City, "In order to rid the town of all useless, disloyal and treacherous persons ... I do hereby strictly order all persons who have refused to enrol their names in the militia lists and to take up arms to quit the town in four days together with their wives and children under pain of being treated as rebels or spies."[4]

But the people of Quebec were not as sympathetic toward the American cause as Carleton feared. They might be opportunistic — many had sold the American Army beef and other goods during their occupation of Canada — but as soon as the American's cash ran out, the habitants refused them credit. And when the army retaliated by raiding farms and capturing supply wagons to take what they needed, they lost any Canadian sympathy they might have gained.

When Montgomery arrived outside Quebec on November 17, 1775, he was met by a second American force. Benedict Arnold had finally arrived in Canada, but his force of 1,500 had been halved by disease and desertion. A dearth of supplies and the arduous journey they had undertaken to get to Quebec had destroyed the spirits of the remainder. This was not the quick thrust into Canada that George Washington had envisioned when he pitched his plan to congress,

> I am now to inform the Honourable Congress that, encouraged by the repeated declarations of the Canadians and Natives, and urged by their requests, I have detached Col. Arnold, with one thousand men, to penetrate into Canada by way of Kennebeck River, and, if possible, to make himself master of Quebeck ... I made all possible inquiry as to the distance, the safety of the route, and the danger of the season being too far advanced, but found nothing in either to deter me from proceeding, more especially as it met with very general approbation from all whom I consulted upon it ... For the satisfaction of the Congress, I here enclose a copy of the proposed route.[5]

The "straight line of two hundred and ten miles" was actually more than twice that length and passed through a rough tangle of woods and swamps that forced the troops to travel a winding route. The falls and carrying places they encountered were neither small nor short. Worse than the hardships offered by nature was the fact that the area was still a virtual no man's land, unsettled and unmapped. There would be no villages or settlements where the soldiers could regroup and replenish their supplies. Arnold and his 1,500 men had no idea what they would face when they set out from Boston with their heavy canoes laden with supplies. The plan had called for Arnold's force to move through the Kennebec Valley to the Chaudière River and then on to the St. Lawrence. But the Kennebec River was a virtually unnavigable morass of rocks and rapids, and the tributary they were to follow, known as the Dead River, was even worse. The aptly named Chaudière

CANADA UNDER ATTACK

(boiler) was equally unfit for navigation. The soldiers were frequently forced to carry their canoes overland and on many days they could only cover a mere five kilometres.[6] "Our march has been attended with an amazing deal of fatigue … I have been deceived in every account of our route, which is longer and has been attended with a thousand difficulties I never apprehended,"[7] Arnold wrote.

Arnold and his men struggled to control their canoes in the churning water. At one point a flash flood destroyed many of their supplies and canoes. By the time they reached the Chaudière a full third of their number had turned back and many of their canoes had been lost or abandoned in the thick swamp and bush of their latest portage. An attempt to float their supplies down the Chaudière on rafts had resulted in the loss of both provisions and ammunition, and the soldiers were forced to eat their shoe leather and the few dogs that had accompanied them, in order to survive.

"We had all along aided our weaker brethren," Private George Morison recorded in his journal, "but the dreadful moment had now arrived when these friendly offices could no longer be performed. Many of the men began to fall behind, and those in any condition to march were scarcely able to support themselves, so that it was impossible to bring them along; if we tarried with them we must all have perished."[8]

By the time Arnold and his men appeared on the Plains of Abraham on November 14, their numbers had dwindled to a little over 700. The remaining men were starved and sickened by the arduous journey. The fact that they had persisted in the face of such adversity and such horrific conditions hardened their resolve. Arnold himself was still determined to take Quebec, and with typical bravado sent a white flag of truce into the city to demand its immediate surrender.

With Carleton still not yet arrived from Montreal, command of the Quebec garrison was in the hands of Lieutenant-Colonel Allan MacLean, who had arrived a mere two days ahead of Arnold and was greeted by a city full of fear and pessimism. The lieutenant-governor, Hector Cramahé, was terrified by the sight of Arnold's force. There was talk of immediately lowering the flag even before Arnold sent his demand for the city's surrender. MacLean, a gruff Scotsman, angrily took control and refused to open the gates to admit the flag of truce. There would be no more talk of defeat.

With no cannon or heavy guns, Arnold was in no position to force the issue and MacLean kept his men well within the protections of the city walls. After waiting for a few days, Arnold withdrew his men to Pointe-aux-Trembles to wait for reinforcements from Montgomery. Montgomery finally arrived on December 2, with 500 troops and supplies. Three days later the combined forces once more stood on the Plains of Abraham. As Wolfe's right-hand man, Carleton knew first-hand the dangers in leaving the safety of the walls of the city to engage the enemy; he had no intention of repeating Montcalm's mistake. For almost 30 days the Americans laid siege to the city. When it finally became clear that the Canadians would not venture from the city to lift the siege, Montgomery and Arnold decided to lift it themselves.

As had happened to Wolfe during his siege, winter was approaching and the Americans were ill-prepared to survive a lengthy wait in the midst of a cruel Canadian winter. They had another incentive though: over half of Montgomery and Arnold's men were due to be released from their service on January 1. It was unlikely they would agree to stay. Morale was low, conditions were horrible, and it was believed that few would voluntarily stay to fight a war on foreign soil. An American deserter came to Quebec and told James Bain, captain of the British militia, about the dispirited state of the attacking army. The man claimed that all the people from the old country wished to be at home and that they had no wish to attack the town. Their leaders were eager to act before more men deserted.

On December 31, in the midst of one of the raging snowstorms that Quebec City is famous for, the Americans launched their attack. Two regiments launched feint attacks on the Plains of Abraham with the goal of distracting Carleton's men from the real invasions being lead separately by Montgomery and Arnold. Arnold's role was to advance along between St. Charles and the Plains in order to storm the Lower Town. From there he and his men would make their way through the mazes of houses, wharves, and storehouses toward the gate that lead into the more heavily fortified Upper Town. They believed that if they could

CANADA UNDER ATTACK

Library and Archives Canada

reach the gate they could easily breach its defences. Montgomery's role was to take the higher route into Lower Town, which would take his troops between the cliffs of Cape Diamond and the St. Lawrence.

Observing the assault from behind the walls of Upper Town, Carleton dispatched a troop of 400 men, under MacLean, to attack the rear of Arnold's troops. Arnold's men waded through knee-deep snow, many of them wearing tiny slips of paper pinned to their hats that read "Liberty or Death." They took the first battery they encountered but Arnold was wounded in the effort and carried out of the battle. His men were quickly stalled at the second battery where they also faced a deep trench dug to prevent their forces from entering Upper Town. Then the boom of cannon and musket fire sounded behind them. MacLean had arrived.

Attack on Quebec by General Montgomery, Morning of 31st December, 1775.

THE FOURTEENTH COLONY

The image is credited: *Library and Archives Canada*

The Americans began to fall like toy soldiers as their enemies fired at them from ahead and behind. There was nowhere for them to go. By the time the barrage lessened enough for them to surrender, nearly 100 Americans had been killed or wounded by enemy fire and dozens of others had drowned while trying to flee across the lightly frozen river. Another 400 American troops were taken prisoner, nearly every remaining member of Arnold's regiment.

Montgomery had his own problems. Several entrenchments had been layered between the cliffs and the St. Lawrence River. In the midst of the fog of musket and cannon fire, Montgomery and his men were unable to see that the enemy entrenchments were only lightly defended by the handful of troops that Carleton thought he could spare. Like Arnold, Montgomery breached the first with relative ease. But in leading the charge to the second, Montgomery and many of his senior officers were killed. The remainder of the soldiers panicked and fled. Carleton, who reported a mere six of him men killed and barely a score wounded, wisely refused to pursue the retreating Americans, choosing instead to stay behind his walls and wait for the anticipated reinforcements he expected to arrive in the spring.

Despite these humiliating defeats, Arnold steadfastly refused to lift the siege and began to prepare to spend the winter outside the walls of Quebec. Plagued by near continual desertions, he sent to Congress for reinforcements hoping they would arrive before expected reinforcements arrived from Britain. In the interim, both sides made occasional forays against each other as pockets of militia stationed outside the fort from both sides engaged. But these skirmishes had little effect on the siege.

Congress did not want to give up their pursuit of the 14th colony any more than Arnold did. In a third open letter to the inhabitants of Quebec, published on January 25, 1776, they assured the Canadians that, "We will never abandon you to the unrelenting fury of your and our enemies; two Battalions have already received orders to march to Canada."[9] Reinforcements did arrive, although among the Americans they were greatly reduced by a smallpox epidemic that was rapidly sweeping through the ranks. Arnold, still wounded, was sent to Montreal where he found growing resentment toward the American presence.

Montgomery had left Montreal in the command of Brigadier-General David Wooster. At first, the general had established good relations with the population, but the relationship slowly eroded as Wooster arrested Loyalists and threatened the arrest of those with Loyalist leanings. He imprisoned a number of local militia who had refused to give up their commissions, and completely disarmed several communities who he suspected of being potentially disloyal. Faced with this growing resentment and the very real possibility of an insurrection, the Americans sent Wooster to Quebec City and replaced him with Arnold. They also sent a delegation to Quebec City, consisting of a Catholic priest and a French printer from Philadelphia, who would be transported to Canada and given monies to re-establish himself, his family, and business there. In exchange, the printer would use his print shop to help promote American interests in Canada. Three members of congress, including Benjamin Franklin, rounded out the delegation. Their mission was primarily one of public relations, to extend the message of common ground to the French Canadians and to assure them that their rights would be protected. The delegation was also granted the funds to raise several regiments from among the French Canadians, who they expected would embrace their cause. Unfortunately, most of their money was paper — Continental Money — which the French Canadians were rejecting from the American Army; the French preferred gold.

What Franklin and his fellow commissioners discovered in Quebec dismayed them. He informed Congress that it was

> impossible to give you a just idea of the lowness of the Continental credit here from the want of hard money and the prejudice it is to our affairs … The Tories will not trust us a farthing … Our enemies take advantage of this distress to make us look contemptible in the eyes of Canadians who have been provoked by the violence of our military in exacting provisions and services from them without pay and conduct towards a people who suffered us to enter their country as friends that the most urgent necessity can scarce excuse since it contributed much to the change of their good dispositions towards us into enmity and makes them wish our departure.[10]

Franklin and his fellow commissioners were pestered with demands for reimbursement so that it was impossible for them to deliver their intended message. In a final and ominous report to Congress they were blunt in their assessment of the situation in Quebec. If Congress could not find the cash to support the army in Quebec, they had better withdraw it before the "inhabitants are become our enemies."[11] Franklin's was not the only voice pleading for help. Schuyler entreated congress to send his suffering armies in Quebec "powder and pork"[12] and both he and Franklin warned Congress that necessity was forcing the armies to go into debt, a debt that had climbed to well over $10,000.

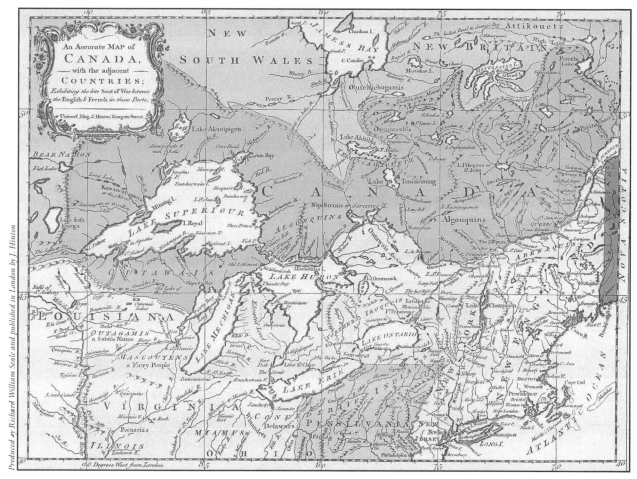

Produced by Richard William Seale and published in London by J. Hinton

There was worse news for the American delegation. Despite the support of the priest who accompanied them, the influential Catholic clergy refused to support their cause, pointing out that the Quebec Act had already given them what they wanted. The French printer had not yet been able to print anything that could be used to sway the populace. Then came the devastating news that the American Army at Quebec City was in a panicked retreat. British ships had been sighted coming up the St. Lawrence, bringing thousands of reinforce-

Reproduction of a 1761 map: "An Accurate Map of Canada with the Adjacent Countries."

ments. After 11 days in Montreal, the venerable Ben Franklin, who had never before shied from controversy or hardship, decided that the problems in Quebec were too many and too complicated for his mission to fix and returned to New York.

In the meantime, Carleton hastily gathered his reinforcements to chase down the retreating Americans. There were several pitched battles at Les Cèdres, Quinze-Chênes, and Trois-Rivières, which all ended with American losses. On May 6, 1776, a large contingent of British reinforcements arrived at Trois-Rivières, undetected by the Americans who occupied Sorel, a few kilometres upriver. The Americans, believing that Trois-Rivières was being held by only a small contingent of British soldiers, raided the settlement. Not only were they unaware of the strength of the British garrison there, they were also wholly ignorant of the terrain. After slogging through a thick swamp, the American troops emerged to face a huge force of British regulars. The Americans scattered back into the swamp. Two hundred American soldiers, including most of the senior officers, were captured. Carleton refused to press his advantage and did not take his troops up the St. Lawrence to make a play for Quebec until the middle of June. He found Sorel abandoned.

Even Arnold was ready to give up. "Let us quit and secure our own country before it is too late,"[13] he wrote. On May 15, he and the American Army, which numbered more than 5,000 in and around Montreal, first attempted to burn down the city then abandoned it and began their retreat back through the Richelieu River to Lake Champlain. They took refuge at Île-aux-Noix but were promptly ousted by the British. At Fort St.-Jean they managed to get away only moments before the British forces arrived. Throughout the summer and into the fall of 1776, Arnold managed to hold the British at bay with a fleet he had built up after his initial taking of Crown Point in 1775, but was finally defeated on October 11, and forced to withdraw from that fort to Ticonderoga. Carleton decided that the Americans were too strong to oust and he contented himself to wait at Crown Point. Finally, on November 2, he pulled his troops from Crown Point and withdrew to spend the winter in Quebec.

The campaign to capture Quebec was an unmitigated disaster for the Americans. Not only had they failed in their attempt to take Canada by force, but they had also failed to convince the Canadians that their future could be secured by uniting with their rebellious neighbours to the south. It would be many years before relationships along the border were sufficiently repaired. The only saving grace for the Americans was that Arnold's tiny naval fleet had held off the British long enough that it had discouraged a full-scale British invasion along Chesapeake Bay, which might have ended the entire revolution. The Americans made one last attempt to secure Quebec at the Paris Peace Conference, which created the United States of America. American negotiator Ben Franklin suggested that all of Quebec be ceded to the Americans, but in the end they received only the Ohio territory.

CHAPTER FIVE:
THE NOOTKA CRISIS

Canada's eastern colonies were not the only ones to capture the attention of foreign armies. By the late 1700s five nations had turned their attention to the westernmost end of Canada, led in part by a desire to exploit the rich store of furs there and by a desire to locate the infamous Northwest Passage. The American interest was still muted by the effort and expense they were already expending on settling their own West. Still, John Jacob Astor and others were making plans to establish trading posts along the Columbia River, and American ships were frequenting the Canadian west coast.

Russia's interest in Canada's west coast was primarily incidental and far less acquisitive than the other nations believed it to be. They made frequent forays into what is now known as the province of British Columbia, but their interests were primarily trade related. On the other hand, the Spanish had made their intentions quite clear. The entire North American Pacific coast, including the island of Vancouver, belonged to them. The British were more recent converts to the practice of exerting their territorial rights over the Pacific coastal regions of Canada, but they were enthusiastic. They had seen the rich stores of fur that could be found in the region and with a new market for furs opening in China, they were eager to exploit the Pacific area. Finally, there were the Nootka[1], who had been there all along and watched the struggles for their territory with interest while they traded with each of the rival nations. The Nootka were well practised in the art of war so it is unlikely that they were perturbed by the arrival of so many foreigners on their shores.

The area at the centre of all of these claims was a series of inlets along the rugged western edge of Vancouver Island, known as Nootka Sound. An early resident of the area captured its rugged, dangerous beauty:

On the ocean coast outside, between the entrances to the great inlets the line of the shore there is broken by low headlands which project from the seaboard, and appear, with their shapeless, out-lying rocks, not unlike the shattered angles of a fortified work; between these capes are narrow beaches, backed by a curtain of rock, over which hill upon hill appears, woody and ragged. As the coast lies exposed to the uninterrupted western swell of the North Pacific, the waves are generally large, and even in calm weather they break with noise on the shore and roar among the caverns. [2]

Friendly Cove was a natural harbour within the Sound, one of very few along the uninviting shoreline. It served as the perfect vantage point for anyone wanting to make forays into the Pacific west coast of Canada and offered immediate access to the Pacific Ocean and the rich developing markets of the Far East.

The Spanish claim to the Pacific Northwest was initiated in the 15th century with a papal bull that had divided the western hemisphere between the Spanish and Portuguese and gave the entire New World to the Spanish. The Spanish bolstered their claim to the region by pointing out that Vasco Núñez de Balboa had laid claim to all the shores touched by the Pacific Ocean when he had crossed the Isthmus of Panama in 1513. Subsequent explorations by other Spanish explorers were used to cement the Spanish claim to the Pacific Northwest.

James Cook was the focus of the British claim. He had made an extensive exploration of the area of Nootka Sound in 1778, but had made no formal claim of sovereignty over it. He did spend a little over a month in Nootka Sound repairing his ships the HMS *Resolution* and the HMS *Discovery*. He may not have laid claim for the British but he did, perhaps inadvertently, encourage an imperialist interest in the region. When they were published in 1784, Cook's extensive journals aroused an intense British interest in the area's rich fur trade. Interestingly, one of the gifts provided to Cook by the Nootka was a set of two silver spoons that looked suspiciously Spanish in origin and may have been traded up the coast or come from the explorations of Balboa some years earlier.

As early as the 1740s the Spanish began to hear rumours of Russian incursions into the Nootka Sound area. These rumours grew more threatening when it was suggested that the Russians intended to establish settlements in the area to cement their claim. Those rumours, whether true or not, were compounded by the Russian penchant for secrecy and their refusal to confirm or deny the rumours. Since it could take years for information to travel between Russia and its isolated Alaskan outposts, it is possible that even they did not know for sure. As a response to potential Russian settlement of the area, in 1774 the Spanish sent the explorer Juan Pérez, along with a Spanish frigate called the *Santiago*, to secure their claim. Pérez's instructions were to travel to 60° north (which is near the site of present-day Cordova, Alaska) and to ascertain the extent of Russian settlements and British incursions in the area. He was also given instructions to land in order to cement Spanish rights to the area, and to treat any Natives he encountered with respect to secure their co-operation. Once on land, according to instructions preserved in the diary of Pérez's companion, Friar Thomás de la Peña, he was to establish the Spanish presence by "using the standard form attached to his instructions, and erect a large wooden cross supported by a cairn of stones hiding a glass bottle, stoppered with pitch, containing a copy of the act of possession signed by the commander, chaplain, and two pilots, 'so that in future times this document will be kept and will serve as an authentic testimony.'"[3] Pérez reached the southernmost tip of the Queen Charlotte Islands, but he turned back while still several hundred kilometres from his destination because of his own ill health and illness among his crew. He had seen several Haida but had not landed or made contact with them.

In 1788, an entrepreneurial British lieutenant named John Meares purchased two ships and decided to pursue these possible riches. He sailed under the Portuguese flag since the only British ships legally allowed to sail the Pacific were those sailing with licenses provided by the South Sea Company or the East India Company. At Friendly Cove, Meares encountered the Nootka chief, Maquinna, who he later claimed had sold him an acre of land and agreed to give him a monopoly on the fur trade in the area. Maquinna would later deny both, but he did allow

The Launch of the North West America at Nootka Sound, 1790.

Meares to erect a small house on the island and to complete work on a new ship that Meares would christen the *North West America*.

Between the voyages of Cook and Meares, hundreds of British, Spanish, American, and Russian vessels had ventured into Nootka Sound in search of furs and other valuables. Their relationship with the Nootka was friendly although businesslike, with one notable exception. In August 1785, a ship captained by James Hanna arrived in the Sound. While the Nootka chief Maquinna visited the

CANADA UNDER ATTACK

The Armourer's Escape

By the turn of the 19th century, Chief Maquinna had helped establish a vibrant trade relationship between his people and the Europeans. But his relationship with the Europeans was not always cordial. In the spring of 1803 an American trading ship, the Boston, arrived in Nootka. The ship's captain insulted Maquinna by suggesting that the gift of a musket the chief had complained was defective had, in fact, been broken by the chief himself. The captain did not realize that Maquinna spoke English, but a blacksmith employed on the ship, John Jewitt, knew immediately that the chief had understood the insult.

A furious Maquinna attacked the ship and slaughtered most of the crew, sticking their heads on pikes around the ship. Jewitt was spared because of his skills as a blacksmith and another survivor was spared when Jewitt claimed the man was his father and threatened to kill himself if he was harmed. Despite the fact that many in the tribe would have preferred him dead, Jewitt spent three years with Maquinna and his tribe, initially as a slave and later as an adopted member of the tribe, slowly accepting their customs and even marrying and fathering a child. But even while he reluctantly became a part of the tribe, Jewitt longed for home and during trading expeditions with other tribes he wrote and left letters in the hopes that they would be relayed to a potential rescuer.

Finally, in 1806, another American ship arrived in the bay. Some of the chiefs thought that Jewitt, a witness to the massacre and a potential liability for the tribe, should be killed or at the very least taken kilometres from the shore and the rescue ship. Instead, Maquinna insisted that Jewitt write him a letter of introduction. Even while he assured the chief he was writing an introduction, Jewitt was writing a warning to the captain that immediately after reading the letter he should take Maquinna captive.

Within hours, Maquinna was in chains and Jewitt was safe on the American ship. In recognition of Maquinna's protection of him over the last few years, Jewitt argued that the chief be released unharmed. Jewitt himself returned to the United States where he published two books and a play about his adventures.

ship, a practical joker ignited a bag of gunpowder placed beneath his seat. Maquinna's injuries were more to his pride than to his physical well-being, but the Nootka were nonetheless furious and attacked the ship. Hanna and his crew barely escaped; their days of trading with the Nootka were over.

During the winter of 1788–89, Meares wintered in China, where he and his partners established a company, the Associated Merchants Trading to the Northwest Coast of America. They gathered a fleet of ships under the command of James Colnett and instructed him to establish a permanent fur trading post at Nootka Sound. The ships in their fleet included the *North West America*, the *Princess Royal*, and the *Argonaut*. Also in 1789, still worried about the Russians, the Spanish laid plans to send Esteban José Martínez to establish some semblance of a permanent settlement at Nootka Sound. Martínez was given two ships to secure the coast: a warship, the *Princessa*, and a supply ship, the *San Carlos*. When Martínez arrived in Nootka Sound on May 5, 1789, he encountered two American ships. The captains quickly informed him of Meares's activities and of the presence of another ship, the *Iphigenia*, flying a Portuguese flag but manned by an entirely English crew. Martínez tracked down the *Iphigenia*, captured her, and arrested her crew and captain, William Douglas. After a few days Martínez released the ships and its crew, instructing them never to return to the area. They complied but more British ships were already on the way.

On June 8, the *North West America* sailed smoothly into Nootka Sound, completely oblivious to the events that had occurred just over a month before. Martínez seized that ship too, on the pretext that he was owed money by Meares' company for the supplies he had given to the *Iphigenia* before he had sent it on its way. The *North West American*, renamed the *Santa Gertrudis la Magna*, was refitted and its command was given to one of Martínez's subordinates, who promptly sailed his prize south to Mexico. A few weeks later, Martínez performed an elaborate ceremony staking Spain's claim to the region and forced the British and Americans to participate. On July 2, two more of Meares' company ships arrived. The first, the *Princess Royal*, was ordered to turn back to China and never return. The second, the *Argonaut*, was seized by Martínez after its captain

CANADA UNDER ATTACK

shouted insults at the Spanish. Its crew and the Chinese workers on board were all arrested. Maquinna and another Nootka chief named Callicum arrived in his war canoe to protest Martínez's treatment of the British, with whom Callicum and the Nootka had enjoyed lucrative trade. Martínez fired his pistol to warn off the chief. One of the Spaniards, who believed his leader had missed, fired and killed Callicum. Maquinna and the remainder of his tribe fled to the other side of the island.

When Martínez discovered that the *Argonaut* also carried the equipment and materials needed to establish a permanent British trading post on the island, he was furious. This was, in his estimation, a direct violation of Spanish sovereignty.

The Spanish Insult to the British Flag at Nootka Sound.

Martínez decided to use the supplies and workers brought by the *Argonaut*. He had the Chinese workers construct Fort San Miguel on Hog Island to guard the mouth of Nootka Sound. On July 4, the American ships fired two salvos in recognition of their independence from Britain and the Spanish returned their salute from the fort.

The *Princess Royal* defied Martínez' instructions and returned to Nootka Sound on July 12. The ship's captain, Thomas Hudson, had not intended to enter the Sound but his ship was becalmed and the Spaniards quickly boarded and took control of the ship.

Despite the friendly relationship between the Spanish and early American arrivals in the Sound, two ships that arrived late in the summer were attacked. The *Fair American* was boarded and captured, the *Eleanora* barely escaped. Then, just as suddenly as he had been ordered to occupy the Nootka Sound, Martínez was ordered to leave and return to Mexico, abandoning all of his fortifications. Martínez found himself out of favour with the new Spanish military command in the Pacific, and when a new expedition, the largest ever mustered by the Spanish in the northwest, arrived in Nootka Sound in the spring of 1790, he was not among them.

Also that spring, Meares returned to England where he quickly whipped up anti-Spanish sentiment over the seizures of his ships and nationalistic fervour over his claim to have settled the Sound first. Public outcry forced a government response and then British Prime Minister William Pitt the Younger announced that British ships had the right to trade wherever they chose, regardless of what Spanish law might have to say about it. The comments were inflammatory and could very well have led to war. The British Navy began to prepare and Parliament took up the cause. Fleets of warships were sent from both Spain and Britain and war would likely have been inevitable had they encountered one another. Luckily they did not. The governments of both nations then called upon their network of alliances for support. The Dutch sided with the British and sent a fleet to their aid, as did the Germans. The Spanish were closely allied with the French and dependent on their response. But although the French did mobilize their navy, in August they announced that they would not go to war.

CANADA UNDER ATTACK

While the posturing and sabre rattling was still going on, another Spanish expedition, this one on a scientific mission under the command of Alejandro Malaspina, arrived in Nootka Sound and mapped some of its inlets. Two of Malaspina's lieutenants took the opportunity to travel into the interior to meet with Maquinna and repair Spanish relations with the chief and the Nootka. Fortunately for Spain, they were successful. Shortly after the Spanish left, two American traders also arrived and secured several deeds to land on Nootka Sound. Generations of their heirs would unsuccessfully press the U.S. Congress to pursue their claims.

Without their French allies, the Spanish decided to press for terms and in 1790 the first Nootka Convention was signed. Under the terms of this first convention, the northwest coast would remain open to traders from all nations, captured British ships would be returned, British prisoners released, and reparations made by Spain for the cost of British losses in Nootka Sound. They were initially unable to come to terms over who had laid claim to Nootka Sound first. For several years the Spanish maintained their fort on Hog Island. The British still backed Meares' claim but the Nootka, won over by Malaspina's officers, denied selling him any land. The two sides decided to meet in Nootka Sound to continue their negotiations. For their representative the Spanish chose Juan Francisco de la Bodega y Quadra, a naval office. The British sent another naval office, George Vancouver. Although friendly, the two men could not agree to terms. Both wanted access to the Columbia River and the Spanish insisted on retaining control of Nootka Sound, something Vancouver could not accept. In the end, both countries agreed to abandon the territory they had tried so hard to acquire. The Spanish fort was handed over to the British but either country could visit the area and trade as they wished. The two also agreed to jointly prevent any other nation from laying claim to the area. Of course, that was not the end of the struggles to control Nootka Sound. Much later, once they had secured Spanish interests in the Pacific Northwest, the Americans tried, again unsuccessfully, to lay claim to the area. The Russians would never venture south of Alaska, but the British would come again, from the Pacific and over the mountains.

CHAPTER SIX:
THE WAR OF 1812

Their claim to the Canadian Pacific thwarted, the Americans had once again decided to "rescue" the inhabitants of central Canada. In 1812, Thomas Jefferson declared to the American people that capturing Canada would be, "a mere matter of marching." Between 1812 and 1814, the Americans launched several ill-fated attacks on Canadian soil: on Montreal, Niagara, Erie, and dozens of other towns, villages, and forts. The Canadians and British were vastly outnumbered — in most cases two to one — yet they still remained unbowed. Even after what the Americans believed would be a symbolic death blow — the razing of York — the Canadians still refused to give up. The "march" lasted for two years but Canada eluded capture and fought back — eventually taking the war to the steps of the White House before the American government finally sued for peace.

For most of the 10 years that Major-General Sir Isaac Brock had been stationed in Canada, he had wanted nothing more than to leave. The career soldier yearned to be where the real action was — on the battlefields of Europe, fighting Napoleon. But instead he was stuck in Fort George, an old wooden fort outside the town of Newark, Upper Canada (present-day Niagara-on-the-Lake, Ontario), waiting for a war that might never happen. He had sent several letters to the Prince Regent — the head of the British armed forces — requesting permission to return to England, but to no avail. His boredom and frustration with life on the Niagara frontier is reflected in a letter he wrote to his brother in 1811: "You who have passed all of your days in the bustle of London, can scarcely conceive the uninteresting and insipid life I am doomed to lead in this retirement."[1]

Blonde, blue eyed, and well over six feet tall, Brock was a dashing figure in his scarlet uniform. At 42, he was the commander in chief of all the troops in Upper Canada. He had proved himself in battle and was respected and admired by his men. In the early 19th century, Canada, then known as "the Canadas," was a loose confederacy of villages scattered along the eastern half of the continent in two provinces, Upper Canada and Lower Canada. Most of the colonials were farmers, and many were recent immigrants from the United States — Loyalists who had fled following the American War of Independence. The fluid border that had been drawn after that war was still defended by a series of isolated wooden forts, most of which were in a state of frightening disrepair. The British soldiers who manned them buffered their isolation with rum and dreams of past victories. The Canadian militia was a largely ad hoc force. They met once a year for training, were seldom available during harvest or other critical times for their farms, and received no pay. Few of the British officers expressed confidence in the abilities of the militia and many were concerned that the Canadians — many of whom were recently arrived immigrants from the United States — could not be counted on in the event of a war with their former country. In fact, Brock's commander, Lieutenant-Governor Sir George Prevost, referred to them as, "a mere posse, ill-arm'd and without discipline."

When a letter arrived from the Prince Regent in early 1812, finally granting Brock permission to return to England, he should have been ecstatic. His opportunity had arrived. Fame and glory in the fight against Napoleon could be his. But, by that time, things had become a whole lot more exciting in Canada. Every sign pointed to war with the Americans, and Brock, as the acting political administrator of Upper Canada, felt duty bound to stay. His next letter to England requested leave to remain in Canada. The colonials had whispered of war with the Americans for most of the decade, but recent rumours seemed to hold more substance. Some members of the American Congress were openly calling for war. Indeed, many of them believed that a war with Canada would barely be a war at all. The odds did seem to be in the Americans' favour; America's population was seven million, it had a trained army of more than 35,000, and an ample supply of arms. By contrast, Canada's population was barely half a million, it had only 5,000 British soldiers, a possible 4,000 militia, and very few arms.[2]

CANADA UNDER ATTACK

All able-bodied Canadian men could have been called up to serve on the militia, but Brock thought it prudent to arm a mere 1,500 of them. He knew that few had any deep attachment to Britain, and fewer still could be counted on to commit to a war they saw as a fight between the British and Americans. Brock had little respect for the Canadian militia. He believed that they were ill-trained and ill-equipped, and that they would desert at the first opportunity. However, the general's opinion about Canadian fighting men would change over the next few months.

On June 19, 1812, while at a formal dinner with his American counterparts at Fort George, Brock was informed that President Madison had declared war on Canada. The officers, who had frequently socialized until then, politely finished their meal before returning to their respective headquarters to plot strategy. The whispers of war became a deafening shout as word spread. No one doubted the outcome. Canadian politicians, civilians, and the Native peoples believed an American victory was inevitable. Brock desperately needed the Natives as allies, but they were reluctant to back the losing side.

No one, it seemed, had counted on Isaac Brock.

"Most of the people have lost confidence," he wrote to one of his brothers. "I, however, speak loud and look big." [3]

Isaac Brock was a natural leader with a reputation for boldness and quick thinking. His ability to bluff was legendary. In his youth, he had been challenged to a duel. He had accepted, stating that he would fight the duel, but not at the usual 30 paces. Instead, he and his opponent would fire at each other over a handkerchief. His opponent had quickly backed down. This kind of quick thinking helped Brock to even the odds against the Americans before the first volley had even been fired. As soon as he heard that war had been declared, Brock passed the news on to his commander at Fort Amherstburg, more than 300 kilometres away at the northwest end of Lake Erie. Shortly after Brock's courier arrived at the quiet fort on the banks of the Detroit River, the American schooner *Cuyahoga Packet* blithely sailed past, on its way to Fort Detroit, Michigan. A young French Canadian lieutenant at the fort, Frederic Rolette, ordered a British captain and six sailors into a longboat. The men calmly approached the *Cuyahoga Packet*, boarded her, and told the captain and crew they were prisoners of war. The Americans were stunned — they'd had no idea that war had even been declared.

The capture of the *Cuyahoga Packet* had provided Brock with some critical information. The boat had been carrying correspondence from William Hull, an American general who was slogging his way through the forests of western Michigan, en route to Fort Detroit. Hull, it turned out, was also oblivious of his country's declaration of war.

The correspondence found on the *Cuyahoga Packet* confirmed what Brock had already suspected. Once Hull reached Fort Detroit, he would launch an attack on the village of Sandwich, near Fort Amherstburg. The correspondence also revealed that Hull felt he had greatly overestimated his enemy's strength, and that he was terrified at the prospect of fighting the Native warriors who were aligned with the British. Further, his army was small and demoralized. Brock estimated it would take Hull at least four weeks to reach Fort Detroit, and he planned to pay him a visit there. But first he arranged to deliver a blow to the Americans on another frontier. During the tedious years before the war, Brock had been quietly placing his men in strategic areas so they would be ready for the Americans' opening move. Since that war had been declared, he sent a missive to Robert Dickson, one of his leaders. Dickson, a Scott known as "the red-haired man," had married a Sioux woman. His loyalties were with the Native peoples who had accepted him as one of their own. He considered himself a Sioux warrior.

Dickson and his 250 warriors had already joined a group of pensioned British soldiers at St. Joseph Island in the northern arm of Lake Huron. When they received word from Brock on July 17, the warriors and old soldiers, accompanied by a handful of fur traders, immediately followed his orders. Under cover of darkness, they silently paddled across Lake Huron to Michilimackinac Island. The island, which had been reluctantly abandoned by the British following the American War of Independence, had been crucial to the western fur trade — and would be again. After quietly waking the villagers and taking them to safety, the old soldiers, along with Dickson and his men, confronted Porter Hanks, the American commander. Terrified at the sight of the Native warriors, Hanks immediately surrendered the fort.

For Brock, it was an important moral victory, albeit a bloodless one. The British had won the first battle. It also sent a clear message to the Native peoples: the British were willing to fight and able to win. The distribution of spoils from the capture sent another message: there were rewards to be had if one sided with the British. Despite orders from his superiors to act defensively only, Brock immediately attempted to provoke a fight with General Hull. On August 15, he ordered an artillery barrage of Fort Detroit. Then he audaciously demanded that the Americans surrender. Safe within the walls of the fort with a large contingent of soldiers, Hull, not surprisingly, refused.

Later that night, after the guns had faded into silence, Brock sent the Shawnee war chief Tecumseh and 500 of his warriors across the Detroit River. Once across, they silently surrounded the fort and stayed hidden in the dense forest. With 500 Native warriors, 7000 local militia, and barely 300 regular soldiers,[4] Brock knew his men were hopelessly outnumbered. To compensate, he used the two strategies that he became famous for. First, he ordered the British soldiers to give the militia their spare uniforms. There were not enough uniforms to go around, so they shared them — a bright red jacket here, a pair of white breeches there. Then he invoked the second part of the plan. On the morning of August 16, after leading this ragtag army across the river, Brock organized the men into columns and ordered them to march at twice the usual distance from one another. To the Americans watching from the fort, Brock's troops seemed twice as numerous as they really were.

Brock rode at the head of the line, his great height and red and gold uniform making him an easy target. When an aide suggested that Brock would be safer somewhere within the column, he refused. He would not, he said, ask his men to go where he was not willing to lead.[5] Just as the British came within range of the American guns, Brock veered off and led his men into the safety of a nearby ravine. Remembering Hull's fear of Native warriors, Brock had ordered Tecumseh to parade his troops across a field in full view of the fort immediately after the army and militia had taken refuge in the ravine. The warriors crossed the field, disappeared into the forest, and doubled back to the place where they had begun

The Death of Brock at Queenston Heights.

their march. Then they marched again — and again. General Hull was convinced he was facing 1,500 warriors and over a thousand British regulars.

The terrified Hull, who had his daughter and grandson inside the fort, asked for a three-day truce. Brock gave him three hours, then frightened the hapless general even more by telling him the lie that the Native warriors would "be beyond control the moment the contest commences."[6] Hull immediately surrendered. Brock and Tecumseh rode into the fort side by side. Brock was resplendent in his uniform, and wore a beaded sash — a gift from Tecumseh — tied around his waist. Tecumseh, in his far simpler fringed buckskin, looked equally impressive. Brock had, it is said, gifted Tecumseh with his own military sash. But Tecumseh,

CANADA UNDER ATTACK

with a customary lack of conceit, had given it to another chief, Walk in Water, whom he considered of higher rank than himself.

Brock had won another decisive victory. But such victories would soon be harder to come by. The United States military commanders decided to focus their next attacks on the Niagara Region and in a hard fought battle there, Brock was killed leading his men in a charge up the infamous Queenston Heights. His men rallied at his death and managed to turn the battle around just in time. By that time, the commander was so well respected that men on both sides of the border attended his funeral.

After that, the longest undefended border in the world erupted in flames. Raids were launched and battles fought in numerous towns and forts along the border: Fort Erie, Frenchman's Creek, River Raisin, Brockville, and Ogdensburg. In a victory more symbolic than strategic, the Americans burned down the Canada East capital of York. A few months later, the British and Canadians would launch a retaliatory raid of their own on the American capital of Washington D.C., burning down the White House and forcing the president to flee.

Ordinary Canadians, many of whom had only recently fled the American Revolution as Loyalists, were drawn into the war effort. Homes and farms were looted and served as battlegrounds. In one small house in Brockville, the Americans barged in and demanded to be fed supper. While they ate, the young mistress of the house listened avidly to their conversation and then trudged 32 kilometres through swampy terrain to warn the Canadian commander, Lieutenant James Fitzgibbon, of an impending American attack. Laura Secord is credited with ensuring the success of the Canadian forces at Beaver Dams against a much larger American force.

As the war dragged on, the violence became more pronounced. Atrocities were committed on both sides. In one horrifying incident the entire town of Newark was destroyed in a raid lead by the Canadian traitor, Joseph Willcocks. At dusk on December 10, 1813, Willcocks and his men, accompanied by a few American militiamen, rode into the town of Newark. They were incensed that the American commanders had earlier called a retreat across the Niagara River.

Government of Ontario Art Collection, 621234

C.W. JEFFERYS

The Battle of Lundy's Lane.

As Willcocks and his men surveyed the town, the townspeople were warned to take what they could from their homes and leave. It had been snowing all day and it was bitterly cold. Willcocks started the burn at the home of an old political foe, a Loyalist by the name of William Dickson who had already been arrested. Willcocks carried the firebrand himself. He went upstairs to find the elderly Mrs. Dickson in bed. She was too ill to walk, so he ordered two of his men to carry her outside. The men wrapped the old woman in blankets and set her in a snowdrift. She watched in anguish as Willcocks burned her home to the ground.

CANADA UNDER ATTACK

There were other, equally horrific stories from that night. One young widow with three small children was turned out of her home with nothing but a few coins. After Willcocks's men plundered and torched her home, they took her money as well. In all, 400 women, children, and elderly men were turned out into the snow that night.

William Merritt, the captain of the Provincial Dragoons cavalry unit, had been on an assignment in Beaver Dams that day with British Force Commander Colonel Murray. As they were making their way back home, they saw the eerie orange glow of the fires in Newark. They guessed what had happened and raced to the scene, but they were already too late. Of all the horrifying scenes Merritt had witnessed during this war that was the worst. All that was left of Newark were glowing embers and charred buildings. Of the 150 homes in the town, only one remained standing. The townspeople had crowded into every room until the house could hold no more. Those left outside huddled in the drifts and beneath makeshift shelters. Some, terrified there might be more attacks, had stumbled off into the freezing night to seek shelter at outlying farms.

The streets were scattered with the remnants of a once prosperous town. Furniture, clothing, dishes, and personal treasures were everywhere, all abandoned by people too cold to carry them. The next morning, Merritt and his men found the frozen bodies of the women and children who had been seeking shelter outside the town. They had lost their way in the blackness of the night. As many as 100 women and children had perished that night in Newark — Willcocks had certainly had his revenge. Soldiers and civilians were equally horrified at this atrocity. The burning of Newark, more than any other action in the war, united the Canadian and British troops and the civilians.

On the Atlantic coast the British maintained a tight blockade and Canadian privateers harried the coast, but it was the Americans who dominated the inland water. By 1813, the Americans had Lake Erie in a stranglehold, with a seemingly unbreakable blockade at Amherstburg on the Detroit River. When Sir James Yeo sailed into Lake Ontario to assume his new position as commodore and commander in chief of the British Navy in the Canadian Great Lakes, he immediately decided that he needed to concentrate his attention on Lake Ontario. Lake Erie was expendable, Lake Ontario, which served as a vital supply line for troops on the Niagara frontier, was not. That philosophy left the Lake Erie force chronically short of ships, men, and supplies. The American blockade made the situation much worse. Food supplies at Amherstburg were running out and there was no more money to pay the army. Sailors had been put at half-rations.

The first major attempt by the British to regain control of the lakes ended in defeat at Sackets Harbour. With the American Navy preoccupied with supporting a raid on Fort George, the British commanders saw an opportunity to attack the American naval base at Sackets Harbour. Then they would burn the newly completed American frigate USS *General Pike*. The British lay anchor several kilometres offshore and the soldiers quickly climbed into flat bottom boats to make their way to shore. They'd gone only a little way before Lieutenant-Governor Prevost thought he saw ships in the distance and, fearing the return of the main American fleet, called the men back. It was a false alarm, but Prevost still refused to call on the attack and they waited until morning. This gave the Americans time to call out the militia. What was supposed to be a quick and easy victory for the British had turned into a complete rout.

Finally, the British naval and army commanders at Fort Erie, Robert Barclay and Henry Proctor, felt that they had no choice. Barclay suggested that waiting was still the more prudent approach but Proctor was adamant: they had to break through the American blockade. The battle of Lake Erie raged for four violent hours, with devastating losses on both sides, before the British finally surrendered. For the first time in the over 300 year history of the British Navy, it had been handed a complete defeat of one of its fleets. The American response to the victory was surprisingly understated. "We have met the enemy," wrote Oliver Hazard Perry, "and they are ours." The defeat forced the British and Canadians to abandon Fort Amherstburg, leaving the field open to Indiana Governor William Henry Harrison, who quickly launched an invasion and pursued Proctor all the way up the Thames River. For months to come, the Americans would dominate Lake Erie.

Terrified of losing the Native alliance, the British tried to convince Tecumseh that the British had won the battle of Lake Erie. Tecumseh was no fool. He knew the British had been defeated, and he suspected they were planning to retreat. Retreating from the Americans was unthinkable to the proud chief. But since he was in an alliance with the British he had no choice. On October 5, 1813, while covering the British retreat up the Thames River with the Canadian militia, Tecumseh decided to make his last stand. He positioned his warriors on the far edge of a great swamp, and placed Proctor and his men to the left on some high ground between the Thames River and the swamp. He told the militia to take up a position between the two groups. Reviewing the position of the British, Tecumseh cautioned Proctor to stand firm. Then he returned to the swamp to wait. There was no trace of the compassionate, literate man. With war paint on his face, and hate in his eyes, he was the quintessential warrior. The American troops arrived at the battleground. The two armies faced each other for several hours, barely 275 metres apart, while the Americans formed their lines. Finally, they were ready for combat. One battalion charged the British, and then a group of Kentucky militiamen advanced towards Tecumseh. The hardened men yelled, "Remember River Raisin" — the site of a British-Native victory and a subsequent scalping earlier in the war — as they spurred their horses forward. As Tecumseh had predicted, the horses got bogged down in the thick marsh, and the Americans were forced to continue on foot. Tecumseh's warriors cut them down.

The respite did not last long. The British line had broken and Proctor's soldiers were running for their lives. Tecumseh and his men had been abandoned. Harrison's troops closed in. When the warriors ran out of ammunition they fought on with their tomahawks. Tecumseh's chilling war cry echoed through the forest; then it was silenced. The great chief was never found. It is generally believed the warriors took his body with them when they retreated. There is no official record of Tecumseh's death and no official marker over his final resting place. But to this day the Shawnee elders say they know where he is buried and that the location of his grave has been passed down from one generation of select leaders to the next.

Wherever Tecumseh lies, the hopes of a Native peoples' confederacy were buried with him. The grand alliance between the Native peoples and the British was finished. The last of the nations made peace with the Americans, and the lands that Tecumseh had fought to keep free were sold to settlers. The Native peoples of Tecumseh's generation lived the rest of their lives on small parcels of reserved lands.

— — — —

In the spring of 1813, with their advance into Upper Canada at a standstill, the Americans turned their attention to the less heavily defended Lower Canada. Their aim was to capture Montreal and cut-off the critical British supply line from the Atlantic. They discussed their plans in detail, unaware that Canadian spies were eavesdropping and taking the information back to a young lieutenant-colonel in the British Army. This officer, a French Canadian aristocrat with the imposing name of Charles-Michel d'Irumberry de Salaberry, was aware of every move the Americans made.

The French Canadians were the wild card in the British deck of support. No one was really certain where their loyalty would lie in the coming conflict. The Americans were counting on the French Canadians to support them. They felt the French Canadians were repressed under the British and would be anxious to escape from British "tyranny." But they were wrong. Most French Canadians disliked and distrusted American-style democracy. They were eager to protect their religion, culture, and language and the British had promised that those would all be protected under their administration.

In late September, the Americans began moving their troops into Lower Canada. This time, they had a sophisticated strategy: a two-pronged attack on Montreal. The plan was for one army to march along the banks of the Châteauguay River, while a second, larger force made its way up the St. Lawrence River by boat. The two rivers run parallel to each other: the Châteauguay runs slightly to the south and joins the St. Lawrence a few kilometres south of Montreal. The two armies met near Kahnawake, about 30 kilometres south of

Spies During the War of 1812

During the War of 1812 both the Canadians and Americans relied heavily on spies from both sides of the border. The Canadian "traitor" Joseph Willcocks was one of the most valuable tools in the American spy arsenal. A member of parliament, Willcocks became convinced that Canada was about to fall to the Americans. He offered his services to the American Secretary of War and began to feed him information about British troop movements. Eventually, Willcocks left Canada to join the American Army as a colonel. He recruited a force of Canadians to accompany him and in 1814, 15 of those men were captured by the Canadians and eight were eventually sentenced to hang. After the hanging, they were decapitated and their heads put on display as a warning to other potential traitors. Willcocks was still safely fighting for the Americans. Toward the end of the war he led the Americans in an attack on the undefended village of Newark, which he had previously represented in the legislature. The village was burned to the ground in one of the worst atrocities of the war.

The Canadians had their spies too. While the American General Wade Hampton was leading his 3,000 troops across the New York bush, intent on attacking Montreal, two Canadian farmers were tracking his every move. Hampton knew all about David and Jacob Manning. Early in October 1813, he had approached the brothers hoping to enlist them as spies for the Americans. But his offer had not quite elicited the response he had hoped it would. The Mannings were far more interested in what Hampton revealed about American military intentions than in what he was willing to pay them for their services. When Hampton finally returned to his troops empty-handed the Mannings quietly headed in the opposite direction. Somewhere to the north, Charles-Michel de Salaberry was waiting with his Voltigeurs. From the Mannings he learned that the Americans were massing on the border, he also learned the size of the army and the route they intended to take. The information supplied by the Mannings helped ensure de Salaberry's victory over the vastly larger American troops.

Montreal, to converge on the city. The invasion force was huge — there were more than 10,000 soldiers.

The first army was led by General Wade Hampton. Its primary purpose was to divert attention from the main force that was massing at Sackets Harbour, New York, and preparing to sail up the St. Lawrence. As Hampton's troops headed towards the Canadian border, the spy David Manning counted the guns, wagons, and soldiers. But Manning had more than numbers to report to de Salaberry. To everyone's surprise, he also reported that 1,400 New York militiamen had refused to cross the border into Canada. By U.S. law, militiamen could not be forced to fight on foreign soil. The units from the northern states did not want to fight people they considered neighbours and friends. Nor were they anxious to be out in the elements during the harsh Canadian winter.

Many of the militia who decided to stay with their general were from the southern states. They were poorly clothed and completely unprepared to face a harsh Canadian winter. Manning also learned about the other American force that was heading up the St. Lawrence under the command of Major-General James Wilkinson. De Salaberry was pleased to have learned so much. Hampton, although furious about the loss of so many of his militia, still felt confident about the coming attack. After all, he had more than 4,000 men with him. On September 21, he created a diversion at the town of Odelltown, just inside the Canadian border. The Americans surprised the small group of British soldiers stationed there, killing three and capturing six.

De Salaberry knew that the Americans had crossed into Canada, but the force he commanded was far too small to launch any kind of counteroffensive. The best he could do was keep the Americans contained inside Odelltown. To that end, he sent out small units of Mohawks to intercept the American patrols. One of those units took down an American patrol. Fear of further encounters with the Native warriors kept the Americans inside the town. Thus, they remained ignorant of how very small de Salaberry's force really was. Faced with what they believed would be a long, tough fight, and hampered by a shortage of water, General Wade Hampton once again retreated back across his own border.

CANADA UNDER ATTACK

As soon as de Salaberry's scouts reported that Hampton's forces had abandoned Odelltown, de Salaberry led his men on a forced 24-hour march to the Châteauguay Valley. He knew Hampton would return and would then take his troops along this valley. The Canadians wanted to be there to greet him. De Salaberry left detachments of soldiers along the way to serve as communication outposts. He finally reached the valley, where he set up camp and waited for Hampton. Meanwhile, Hampton had set up camp at Four Corners, a small town just inside the American border at the southern end of the Châteauguay Valley, about 15 kilometres from de Salaberry's camp. When de Salaberry learned of the Americans' whereabouts from his spies, he sent a few units of warriors and Voltigeurs to pepper the encampment with sniper fire. They terrorized the camp every night for two weeks. The Americans were so alarmed that they would not venture outside the encampment at night.

In the meantime, Lieutenant-Governor Prevost, who was in Kingston, had finally realized that Montreal was the Americans' main target. He made plans to take reinforcements to de Salaberry by land. But first he went to one of his officers, Red George Macdonell, and asked him to get his first battalion to de Salaberry as soon as possible. Red George reached de Salaberry on October 24, but his even with his men the Canadians were still outnumbered three to one. Fifteen hundred Canadians speaking French, English, Mohawk, and even Gaelic were facing off against over 4,000 battle-hardened Americans. What de Salaberry needed was an edge. By that time, Hampton's troops were very close. Close enough to see what they thought were hundreds of reinforcements marching towards de Salaberry's camp. De Salaberry had used Brock's ploy of having the same men march back and forth wearing what looked like different uniforms each time. Not actually having any different uniforms, the men just turned their jackets inside out so the white linings showed.

Witnessing a near continuous stream of apparent reinforcements, Hampton was fooled into believing de Salaberry's force was twice the size of his own. Therefore, he dismissed the idea of a head-on assault. Instead, on October 25, 1813, he sent a force of 1,500 men into the forests to attack de Salaberry's flanks. The

Voltigeurs scouts detected them. Red George and his men, along with a group of Voltigeurs, engaged the Americans and fought them off.

That afternoon, Hampton decided he would have to try a head-on assault after all. The American troops advanced toward the ravines. He had an officer call out an offer, "Surrender, we wish you no harm." De Salaberry raised his musket and fired his response. There was a furious exchange of fire and de Salaberry ordered his men to take cover behind the *abatis*. Thinking that the Canadians and British were retreating, the Americans began to cheer.

De Salaberry encouraged his men to return the victory shouts. These shouts came from the top of every ravine. Then Red George's men picked up the shouts from their reserve position in the woods. The Mohawks added to the ruckus with their war whoops. The Americans had stopped cheering. They fired volley after volley into the woods at what they believed to be thousands of warriors. Finally, de Salaberry sent his buglers into the woods to sound an imaginary advance. Silence fell over both armies. De Salaberry called out to one of his Voltigeurs in French, warning him to communicate solely in French so that the enemy would not understand. The man replied that the soldiers who had attacked their flanks that morning had regrouped and were attacking again. De Salaberry told him to draw the fight to the riverbank. When the Americans neared the river, the Canadians sank to their knees and began to fire. The Americans returned fire but the musket balls flew harmlessly over the heads of the Canadians. Of the Canadians aim, an American prisoner would later remark that they were horrifically accurate, few of their rounds failed to hit their mark. From across the river bank, de Salaberry and another corps of Voltigeurs also launched an attack on the hapless Americans. Finally, the Americans sent a messenger to Hampton to request permission to retreat. In the meantime, another American force had gathered in the clearing beneath the *abatis* and was firing ineffectually into the deep shadows of the forest where the ghostly cheers and war whoops from Macdonell's men and the Mohawks still reverberated. Hampton, outsmarted by his enemy once more, ordered a general withdrawal. In the haste to retreat, the American dead and wounded were left in the ravines. De

Salaberry had the American wounded taken to a nearby field hospital, along with his own wounded.

While General Hampton was leading his troops back to the border, the other arm of the American invasion force, 7,000 men strong, was making its way up the St. Lawrence River in hundreds of light river boats. The flotilla made slow progress. From the Canadian side of the river they were bombarded by cannon fire. Their commander, General Wilkinson, was sick and in no state to rally his troops. The soldiers were not in a hurry to go anywhere either. It took eight days for them to cover 130 kilometres. Along the way, the American flotilla stopped to interrogate farmers on both sides of the border, hoping to get intelligence about the British and Canadian forces. The soldiers looted the homes and property of Canadian civilians, earning them the lasting enmity of the local population. When the Americans interrogated them, the Canadians fed them a series of outrageous tales that magnified the strength of everything from the rapids ahead to the size of the army they would face. This time, it was the civilians who tricked the Americans into believing they were up against a huge army. Finally, on November 11, 1813, the American force reached a farm (near the present-day town of Long Sault, Ontario) owned by a man named John Chrysler. They knew they could go no farther by boat until they had disabled the cannons that were still firing at them from the Canadian side of the river. The dangerous Long Sault rapids were ahead, and they could not hope to navigate them while under fire.

The Canadians and British, however, had expected the Americans to stop at Chrysler's farm. They told the Chrysler family to hide in their cellar, and then positioned their troops in the surrounding fields.

As always, the defending army was vastly outnumbered. Therefore, they scattered in small groups: a unit of Voltigeurs in the woods, a unit of Mohawks in a cornfield, and a unit of British regulars beyond the barns. Everywhere the Americans looked, they could see the enemy.

The Americans had already received word of Hampton's demoralizing defeat. When they saw the troops at Chrysler's farm, they realized they would have to engage them. Wilkinson, still too ill to leave his bed, ordered his junior officer to engage the British in a staid military fashion, fighting first one unit and then the next. The officer followed his orders and the effects were debilitating. The Americans were continually harassed; just as they appeared to dispatch one unit of the enemy, another stood up to engage. Finally, Wilkinson called the retreat. The exhausted soldiers willingly piled into their boats and retreated across the river to the American side. The attack on Montreal was a rout.

An equally savage war was being fought on the seas and the Great Lakes. If there is any debate about who won the War of 1812, there can certainly be no doubt as to who won the war on the eastern seaboard. By the time the Treaty of Ghent was signed, troops from Nova Scotia occupied no less than half of the state of Maine. Canadians privateers had captured four times as many ships as their American counterparts and placed a stranglehold on American trade that saw American exports reduced from $45,000,000 before the war to less than $7,000,000 when it ended.[7] And while the Canadian maritime economies enjoyed unprecedented prosperity during and immediately after the war, the American economy suffered a deep recession from which they were very slow to recover. Over the course of the war 41 Canadian privateers ruled the waters between the Maritime colonies and states, taking literally hundreds of American ships as prizes. Nova Scotia, New Brunswick, and Newfoundland thrived on the profits brought in by these ships.

On August 25, 1814, the Canadians and British swarmed into the naval base at Bladensburg, New York, and easily disarmed the militia guarding that entrance to Washington, D.C. By nightfall, the capitol itself had been set afire. Public buildings were looted and documents littered the city streets. While that fire was ravaging the American capital, representatives of Britain and America were meeting in the Belgian town of Ghent to discuss possible terms for peace. As the politicians continued their negotiations, soldiers were fighting more battles on land, lakes, and sea.

By 1814, when the final battle of the war was fought on American soil, near the city of New Orleans, Louisiana, the terms of peace had already been brokered. The war ended with the border much as it had always been. Farmers, merchants, and tradesmen from both countries once again crossed freely to conduct their business. But within Canada, much had changed. For the first time, the country and its people — Native, French, and English — had united against a common enemy and together they had halted a seemingly unstoppable invasion.

CHAPTER SEVEN:
REBELS IN CANADA

With the Americans threat contained, at least for the moment, the Canadian colonies were faced with a new threat. This one was not launched from foreign soil but rose from the centre of the Canadian colonies, fuelled by conflicts of race, economics, and class.

In early November 1837, the threat exploded into war.

— — — —

The men had waited in silence for hours. The sudden peel of the church bells struck terror in the hearts of some, elation in others. Finally, the English had come for them. The words of their *Patriote* leader, Dr. Wolfred Nelson, an Englishmen who had married a French woman and adopted their cause as his own, rang in their ears, drowning out even the steady clang of the bells. "*It is your lives they seek; sell them as dearly as you can. Stay steady, don't drop your powder and attend to your duty — self-preservation.*"

When the first musket fired, it was clear to both the French and English that there could be no turning back. Civil war had begun.

They may not have wanted to become the 14th colony, but that did not mean that Canadians were entirely happy with their government. Upper Canada was controlled by a small, wealthy group known as the Family Compact. In Lower Canada a similar group of elites known as the Château Clique were in control. Resentment simmered as the farmers and soldiers who had fought to protect Canada did not have much say in how they were governed and how their taxes were spent.

Things had started slowly and with little evidence of the violent turn that things were about to take. A tidal wave of revolutions had swept through Europe and one by one the established governments of France, Greece, Belgium, and Poland had fallen; but very little had changed for the residents of Lower Canada. They were still ruled by Britain, which was also the major market for their goods and the source of most of the goods they purchased.

But events soon conspired to change that relationship. Resentment simmered against the ruling elite, most of whom were English. During an election riot in 1832, three Frenchmen were shot and killed by British troops. The repeal of the Corn Laws meant that the Canadians no longer received preferential treatment for their imports or exports. In fact, much of the market in Britain had disappeared. A severe drought added to the misery of the farmers of Lower Canada and they were soon on the verge of starvation. Many lost their farms only to see them bought by new English immigrants, lured by a hierarchy eager to increase the English population of the colony. Worse, the new settlers brought cholera with them and it quickly spread to an already weakened rural French population.

The *Patriotes*, who dominated the Lower Canadian Assembly, adopted a list of 92 Resolutions designed to limit the powers of the unelected, predominantly English upper house, and forwarded it to Britain. For three years the resolutions were ignored by the British. In frustration, the *Patriotes* refused to vote for any money to go toward government supplies and wages, effectively paralyzing the government. Finally, word reached the colonies that the British had rejected the resolutions and instead had adopted 10 separate resolutions, none of which served to change the power structure in Lower Canada. Protests broke out across Lower Canada. Numerous public demonstrations were held, many openly calling for the French to defy their English rulers.

On October 31, 1837, over 5,000 Canadians gathered in Saint-Charles, where Louis-Joseph Papineau called on them to ignore the British resolutions and elect their own governments, judges, and militia officers,

The long and heavy chain of abuses and oppressions under which we suffer, and to which every year has only added a more galling link, proves that our history is but a recapitulation of what other Colonies have endured before us. Our grievances are but a second edition of their grievances. Our petitions for relief are the same. Like theirs, they have been treated with scorn and contempt, and have brought down upon the petitioners but additional outrage and persecution. Thus the experience of the past demonstrates the folly of expecting justice from European authorities. [1]

But others, including Dr. Wolfred Nelson, called for a more violent response. Addressing thousands of supporters he suggested the time for talk had gone, "The time has come," he said, "to melt down our tin spoons and tin plates and forge them into bullets."[2]

The establishment, including the English merchants and the French Bishop of Montreal, listened in horror. The call to arms brought to mind the bloody horror of the French Revolution. In Montreal, frustrated by a government seemingly held hostage by a small group of disgruntled Frenchmen, the English Doric Club members attacked several newspaper offices and ransacked the home of one of the *Patriote* leaders. In response, the *Patriotes* flew into action. Across Quebec they disarmed government supporters, intimidated judges, and attempted to force the local militias to stay neutral in the conflict to come. Revolution, it seemed, was inevitable.

The government response was swift. A list of *Patriotes* was drawn up and troops were dispatched to arrest them and bring them to Montreal for trial. Papineau was warned in time, but many others were not so fortunate. As Papineau fled to the United States, one group of arrested men was rescued by their fellow *Patriotes*, who attacked the convoy of soldiers bringing them in. Within Montreal companies of loyal militia were raised, primarily from amongst the English population, which at that time numbered half the city's population. This freed the army to meet the rebels who were already massing at Saint-Charles. One troop of

300 soldiers departed from Montreal under Lieutenant-Colonel Charles Stephen Gore, determined to head off the rebels.

They marched through the cold, wet snow of a late November storm that turned parts of the road into a pit of mud. As they marched they grew more tired, cold, and hungry. When they reached the village of Saint-Denis on November 23, 1837, they encountered a group of 800 rebels under the command of Dr. Wolfred Nelson. "At long last they came in sight of the place where they would breakfast and where they did breakfast on Powder and ball,"[3] wrote George Nelson. From their barricaded positions on the top floors of the village houses, the poorly armed rebels were able to hit the advancing British troops with deadly accuracy. The peaceful village had been turned into bedlam itself. The church bells rang incessantly, villagers scurried to find shelter, and *Patriote* sympathizers from neighbouring villages streamed in, pitchforks and ancient muskets in hand. The British sank back and loaded their big guns, but even at that great a range, the snipers were able to pick off the gunners while the great guns themselves did scant damage. They were able to take a few houses, but after a pitched battle of over six hours that resulted in British casualties but no discernible movement in position, the British commander ordered a retreat, leaving the cannon behind in their hurry.

The *Patriotes* did not have much time to celebrate their victory. Two days later, on November 25, they were engaged at Saint-Charles under the command of Thomas Storrow Brown. That time the attacking British force was well rested and well-fed. Above all, they were experienced, battle-hardened troops in contrast to the *Patriotes*, who, regardless of their leaders' best attempts, remained an inexperienced, disorganized group. Despite the arrival of over 2,000 *Patriotes* before the British flags were seen on the horizon, fewer than 300 would stay to defend the village. The rest fled once they'd seen the shells from the British cannons levelling the village. There would be no British retreat. The barrage of cannon fire was quickly followed up by a British advance and several rounds of musket fire. Then the order came to fix bayonets. The *Patriotes*, with their ancient muskets and too few bayonets, were at a disadvantage.

In the confusion, a small group of *Patriotes* made the pretence of surrendering and then took direct aim at their captors, killing several. The British, outraged at this breech of military etiquette, retaliated by bayoneting large numbers of *Patriotes* and then looting and burning the village. By the time the fog of musket fire had cleared, 150 *Patriotes* lay dead on the streets of Saint-Charles. The British had suffered a mere three dead and 18 wounded. After the smoke had cleared and the guns had ceased their horrifying tattoo, families arrived to claim their loved ones on the battlefield. Among them were two young girls. They approached a soldier, Captain George Bell, who was standing guard and asked him to help them find their father. They searched among the tangled web of bodies until they found him. Bell recalled that it was a horrible sight; the man's head had been shattered by a musket ball, his body frozen stiff. The girls had brought a sleigh with them and Bell helped them carry their father's body to it and gently covered him as if to ward off the winter cold. The faces of the girls would haunt Bell for the rest of his life, the one unable to shed a tear, betraying none of the emotion she surely felt, and the other, so overcome with grief that she staggered to the sleigh.[4]

The battle of Saint-Charles turned the tide in favour of the British. Prisoners were marched to Montreal in chains, where they were paraded through the streets like trophies. The only disappointment for the British was that the rebel leaders had managed to escape. With the southeastern half of Quebec was secure, the British turned their attention to the area north of Montreal, much of which was still in the hands of the *Patriotes*. Two hundred of them had gathered at the village of Saint-Eustache. Many lacked weapons and when they asked for some so that they might defend themselves, their pragmatic leader, Dr. Jean-Olivier Chénier, replied, "Relax, some will be killed and you will take their muskets."[5] On December 15, Lieutenant-Governor John Colborne ordered his men to surround the village and his artillery to fire on its centre. Then, slowly and methodically the soldiers moved in, vice-like, their muskets blazing, to confront the rebels. They took most of the major buildings, leaving just the church in which the *Patriotes* tried to find refuge. An attempt to take the church was thwarted by *Patriotes* who had taken up position on the church's balcony. Instead, the British soldiers set fire to the church and as the *Patriotes* jumped from the windows to escape the flames they were cut down by British soldiers. Captain George Bell recorded the incident in his journal,

> [T]he priest's house they kept up a brisk fire upon our men. The guns came up to a corner of the main street, and riddled the church door. The Royals then were ordered to storm it (the rectory), which they did in most gallant style, firing the adjoining house, which burned out the rebels there. Under the great column of smoke that issued from this building, many of the enemy escaped from the church, and crossed the river on the ice; but they met the Volunteers who were waiting for them in the wood and were slaughtered. The flames soon communicated to the church. There was but one choice left — to bolt out and be shot, or be burned alive. There was no escape, and they died as they fought, regardless of life. Chenier, the only chief who stood by them to the last, was killed in the churchyard. [6]

When the battle finally ended more than 70 *Patriotes*, including Chénier, lay dead.

But the soldiers were not finished. Together the regulars and volunteers burned down every house in Saint-Eustache that they believed had provided refuge to the rebels. At nightfall they began to loot and pillage the remainder. Even the most battle-hardened soldiers were appalled by some of the cruelty they witnessed, most of which was committed by the volunteers. The volunteers, mostly English, had joined out of loyalty and occasionally fanaticism, and were determined to destroy the French rebels. The regulars were career soldiers who were simply doing their duty. Another group of volunteers arrived the day after Saint-Eustache fell and they amused themselves by looting the neighbouring farms, employing their usual tactic of taking everything they could carry and then making "the men, women and children undress, leaving them virtually naked at the doors of their burning houses."[7]

By that time Colborne had taken the village of Saint-Benoît. He had met no resistance but burned the village to the ground anyway. The village of Saint-Hermas was burned later that same day. Throughout the countryside, houses were searched and *Patriote* leaders captured. The rebellion in Lower Canada seemed to be over.

Word of the rebels' actions in Lower Canada had encouraged those with similar complaints in Upper Canada. For years, American settlers had been pouring into Upper Canada, drawn by the lure of cheap land. By 1812, these "late Loyalists" vastly outnumbered the original Loyalists and despite the fact they had to swear allegiance to the crown no one was quite sure where their sympathies really lay. As in Lower Canada, a small group of elite merchants ruled the city of Toronto, and therefore the province. They controlled the executive council and the finances of the province, and more importantly they were responsible for dissemination of the vast tracts of rich land known as the Clergy Reserves, most of which was tithed to the Anglican Church. Within the legislative council moderate reformers led by men such as Robert Baldwin called for representation by population. More radical reformers, like William Lyon Mackenzie, called for more extensive reforms that would create a social, legislative, and economic structure more like that in the United States. Mackenzie was an influential newspaperman whose newspaper, the *Colonial Advocate*, was the voice of the reform movement in Upper Canada. A brilliant orator, he was elected the first mayor of Toronto. Both Baldwin and Mackenzie were vigorously opposed by the Family Compact as threats to their power. And like in Lower Canada, widespread crop failures and economic difficulties exacerbated the situation.

In 1835 Mackenzie helped draft a list of demands similar to the *Patriotes*'s 92 Resolutions, and sent it to England with a demand that they be immediately implemented; "This country is now principally inhabited by loyalists and their descendants, and by an accession of population form the mother country, where is now enjoyed the principals of a fair and responsible government and we feel that the practical employment of the same system in this part of the empire to be equally our right."[8] Mackenzie also suggested that all confidence has been lost in public offices and councils.

Sir Francis Bond Head was dispatched by Britain as the new lieutenant-governor of Upper Canada in the hope that he could find common ground between the reformers and the establishment and forestall violent clashes of the kind that were threatening Lower Canada. Britain could not have made a worse choice. Bond Head quickly allied himself with the conservative members of the Family Compact. He directly intervened in the election of 1837, helping to ensure that the reformers, like Mackenzie, were evicted from the seats in the legislature and securing those seats for conservatives instead.

With their route to legislative reform blocked, Mackenzie and the other reformers became convinced that the only way they could achieve reform was armed insurrection. Baldwin quit the legislative assembly and attacks were made on Mackenzie's reformist newspaper, the *Colonial Advocate.* At the end of July a group of reformers led by Mackenzie met to write a declaration that was strikingly similar to the one issued by the Americans prior to the American Revolution. In October, Bond Head, in a somewhat arrogant desire to show that all was well in his colony, sent all of his troops to Lower Canada to help quell the rebellion there. Mackenzie saw his chance. When word reached the rebels that the rebellion in Lower Canada had failed, they knew they must act. On December 5, a group of rebels met at Montgomery's Tavern on Yonge Street in Toronto. There they were joined by other reform minded men from the counties. Few had weapons, most carried only their pitchforks and their outrage.

The men marched down Yonge Street toward city hall, where the intended to take control of the rich cache of arms and ammunition stored there. They approached the city just as darkness fell and were challenged by a small group of conservatives led by the sheriff. After firing first on the rebels, the volunteers abandoned their position and ran. The first line of the rebels immediately opened fire and then dropped to their bellies to allow the second line to fire. In the darkness, the second line believed that their entire front line had been killed by the sheriff's men and they too turned and ran. The lines behind them quickly followed suit. The opening move of the rebellion was an embarrassing disaster.

Two days later, Sir Allan Napier MacNab led a regiment of some 900 militia-

CANADA UNDER ATTACK

Government of Ontario Art Collection, 621229

men to Montgomery's Tavern, where they engaged the handful of rebels who had remained with Mackenzie. The battle lasted scarcely half an hour and the majority of the rebels, including Mackenzie, fled to the countryside. The volunteers may have believed that the rebellion was over, but Mackenzie was far from finished. Mackenzie escaped to Niagara and set up camp on Navy Island in the middle of the Niagara River. He promptly renamed the island the Republic of Upper Canada and offered free land to anyone who was willing to join him. On the American side of the river the people were delighted to see such open defiance of British rule. They had heard of Mackenzie, who had openly called for joining Upper Canada to the United States and who frequently referred to Upper Canada as the

The March of the Rebels upon Toronto in December, 1837.

REBELS IN CANADA

State of Upper Canada. The Americans offered to supply the fledgling republic by way of the steamer *Caroline*.

MacNab and his men finally tracked Mackenzie to Navy Island and were outraged when they realized the assistance the Americans were lending the rebels. On December 29, MacNab ordered his naval commander, Andrew Drew, to destroy the *Caroline*. In the dead of night, Drew and his men rowed over to Navy Island but failed to find the ship. They then decided to row across to the American side where they killed a night watchman, set fire to the *Caroline*, and then sent it careening toward the falls. The Republic of Upper Canada was finished. The Americans were outraged. The British claimed the attack on the *Caroline* was a pre-emptive strike while the Americans claimed that such strikes were only legal if circumstance were "instant, overwhelming, leaving no choice for means and no moments for deliberation."[9] On January 9, a group of rebels who had found shelter in Detroit sailed across to shell the town of Amherstburg, but they immediately retreated when challenged by a ship commanded by Upper Canadian Loyalist militia. On January 13, Mackenzie and his men abandoned Navy Island.

Stunned by the insurrections in the Canadas, the British began a buildup of troops in the region. They had been lucky before — the insurrection in the poorly defended colonies could easily have ended very differently. Since ice blocked the St. Lawrence, several regiments were sent on the arduous overland journey from Nova Scotia to Lower and Upper Canada. But soon the St. Lawrence was free of ice. By the middle of 1838 over 10,000 British troops were stationed in the Canadas. Thousands more volunteers had been trained and armed in the militia. They had good reason to prepare. There were rumours of secret societies, populated by escaped rebels and their American sympathizers, who were already organizing another attack on the Canadas.

These secret societies were known as the Hunters' Lodges, complete with secret passwords and signals. By mid-1838 their members were believed to number more than 40,000. Their sole purpose was to drive the British from North American and liberate Canada. The members of the lodges were heavily armed; many of the American members were battle-hardened veterans of the Revolutionary and Civil wars, and the War of 1812. One of their first forays into Canada, on February 28, was led by Wolfred Nelson who crossed the border with 300 men to declare the independence of Lower Canada before fleeing back to the States when the British Army challenged him. Not willing to become involved in another war with the British so soon, the American Army promptly disarmed the would-be rebels as soon as they crossed the border. Sporadic pitched battles were waged on Pelee Island, near Windsor, and in the Niagara Region, but nothing came of them.

But in Lower Canada there were no illusions that the rebels were finished. The government firmly believed that the city was rife with rebels who were simply waiting until the right moment to declare for their cause and overthrow the British. On November 2, the suspected plot was finally uncovered. The *Patriotes* and Hunters were planning to take Sorel and then move on to Forts Chambly and St. Jean. In the meantime, *Patriotes* within the city of Montreal would overcome the British soldiers during Sunday service when they were only permitted to carry bayonets. The city was on high alert.

On November 3, they attempted to cross the border to attack Sorel and several of the other southern parishes but were turned back by the British. On November 5, they managed to make it to Napierville. They quickly spread to control other towns but the British and militia were not far behind. In a three-pronged attack the British took one after another of the villages that the *Patriotes* had so recently taken for their own. First Beauharnois fell, then Saint-Timothée. Lacolle fell on November 7, followed by Odelltown and Baker's Farm on November 9. Finally the troops converged on the final rebel holdout at Napierville. Facing what they thought would be a potential massacre the rebels quickly abandoned the town and fled back across the border.

To the east, the general alarm was sounding as a 400 strong army of well-equipped rebels and hunters entered Canada near Prescott. When he realized he had been spotted and that any attempt to take Fort Wellington would be suicide, the rebel leader Nils von Schoultz withdrew to a windmill just east of the fort. On November 13, shells from two ships moored on the nearby St. Lawrence began to fall on the windmill and some 500 troops advanced to surround it. In the smoke

Library and Archives Canada

**Insurgents at Beauharnois,
Lower Canada.**

CANADA UNDER ATTACK

and confusion of the battle most of the rebels and American volunteers managed to escape back to the United States, but 130 were captured. Twenty militiamen died in the skirmish, along with 30 rebels.

On December 4, the rebels made one last attempt, stealing over from Detroit to capture the city of Windsor. No sooner had they taken possession than a group of loyal militia attacked and forced them to give up the city. Four militiamen and 27 rebels were killed. Upon learning that one of the militiamen who had been killed was his best friend, their commander, Colonel John Prince, ordered five rebels shot on the spot. The rebellions had finally ended.

In the dying days of the rebellions, the Canadas mobilized almost 20,000 volunteers for their defence. Both colonies were paralyzed with fear. Were the insurrections finally over or were the rebels simply in hiding, awaiting their next opportunity to strike? The casualties of the battles in Upper Canada had been relatively light but those in Lower Canada had been devastating. Almost 300 *Patriotes* had fallen, virtually all French Canadian, and with farms and fields scorched and destroyed their families and neighbours were impoverished. A rural constabulary was created in order to repress and rout (often violently) any potential liberal thinkers from among the French population. Thirteen rebels and their American sympathizers were executed in Upper Canada and a further 86 were shipped to Australia. In Lower Canada, 12 *Patriotes* were hung and another 58 were transported to Australia.

The rebels were eventually defeated, but many of their leaders would later became Canada's most prominent politicians — Louis-Hippolyte Lafontaine, William Lyon Mackenzie, Louis-Joseph Papineau, and George-Étienne Cartier to name but a few. In Lower Canada, the rebellions prompted the genesis of French-Canadian nationalism.

While the rebellions may not have succeeded, they lead directly to the Durham Report. John George Lambton, the Earl of Durham, was dispatched to Canada to discover the roots of the Canadian problem and to propose suggestions for reform. What he found there initially surprised him. "I expected," he wrote, "to find a contest between a government and its people: I found instead two nations warring in the bosom of a single state: I found struggle, not of principles but of races."[10] He recommended that the two Canadas be joined into one province and that responsible government, such as that already enjoyed by the British, be put in place. The first recommendation was quickly adopted; the second would take a little longer to achieve but eventually it too would come.

Durham's report aside, the rebellions also served to finally dispel the widespread American notion that Canada was ripe for the taking. The vast majority of Canadians, including those who incited rebellion, had no interest in joining the United States. Their ferocity in defending their country was as unmatchable as it was unbeatable.

CHAPTER EIGHT:
AROOSTOOK — THE ALMOST WAR

We'll feed them well with ball and shot.
We'll cut these redcoats down,
Before we yield to them an inch
Or title of our ground.

— American Fighting Song, Bangor, Maine, 1839

The Americans may have given up on the idea that the Canadians were eager to join them, but that did not mean they'd given up trying to acquire all, or at least part, of Canada, by whatever means necessary.

In 1783 two empires, one old and established the other young and hungry, met in Paris to end the Revolutionary War. Among the items that the British and American representatives debated was who would claim a large tract of land known as the Aroostook Valley. They struggled with Article 2, which was intended to describe the northeastern border of the United States,

> From the northwest angle of Nova Scotia, to wit, that angle which is formed by a line drawn due north from the source of the St. Croix river to the highlands, along the said highlands which divide those rivers that empty themselves into the St. Lawrence, and those which fall into the Atlantic ocean, to the north-western most head of the Connecticut river....

It was an imprecise description to say the least. Both Maine and Britain claimed large, overlapping parts of the territory. But in 1783, the negotiators were unconcerned. The Aroostook was unmapped, sparsely populated, and filled with dense forests that made it barely inhabitable; definitely not something worth fighting for. By 1840, however, the world was a different place. Urbanization and expansion created an insatiable appetite for lumber and the demand reached previously unimaginable levels. Suddenly these vast tracts of forested land became almost as valuable as gold. Just as suddenly everyone wanted the Aroostook. "This whole region is a mighty forest," *The New Yorker* magazine poetically wrote. "The rivers hollow out a path through the trees and the sparse settlements make windows in the broad forest landscape."[1]

An eclectic collection of people populated the area. French Acadians inhabited much of the Saint John and Madawaska river valleys while Americans settled near the Aroostook River. Near the west bank of the Saint John River were the British. The French speaking residents of the Madawaska were technically British subjects, but they felt no allegiance to either the British or Americans. They referred to themselves instead as residents of the *République du Madawaska*. Added into this mix of people were the hundreds of seasonal lumbermen who bedded their farms down for the winter and then polled the Saint John River in search of lumber. Inevitably there were tensions — between the permanent residents and these seasonal entrepreneurs and between the separate encampments of Americans, English, and French.

For more than 100 years, North America had been in a near constant state of war as the European nations battled for control of the continent. By 1814, Britain had emerged as the sole global power and the rebellions had been quelled. The tumultuous relationship between Britain and its former colony, the United States, had calmed. But it would not last. In 1819, John Quincy Adams, then U.S. secretary of state, claimed that

> the world must be familiarized with the idea of considering our proper domination to be the continent of North America. From the time we became an independent people, it was as much a law of nature that this become our pretension as the Mississippi should

CANADA UNDER ATTACK

flow to the sea. Spain has possessions upon our southern border and Great Britain upon our northern borders, but it is impossible that centuries should elapse without finding them annexed to the United States.

A lumber camp in the disputed Aroostock region, January 1854.

In 1840, the Aroostook seemed a good place for them to start that annexation.

For part of the War of 1812, the British had occupied large tracts of land in the Aroostook and Saint John river valleys, intending to annex the lands to Canada once the war ended. But the Treaty of Ghent restored the ambiguous borders of the Treaty of Paris and with it the competing claims of both the U.S. and Britain to the valley. The situation was further exacerbated when Maine gained state-

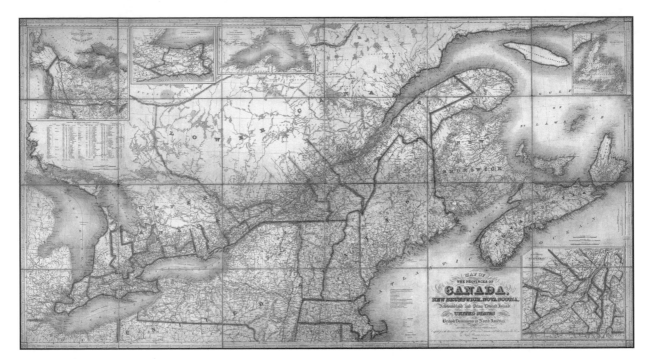

Map of the Provinces of Canada, New Brunswick, Nova Scotia, Newfoundland, and Prince Edward Island, with a large section of the United States and showing the boundary of the British dominions in North America, according to the treaties of 1842 and 1846.

hood in 1820 thereby inheriting the dispute over its northeastern border. The young state was determined to pursue her claim and the riches to be found there. In 1825 a great fire destroyed much of the forests in New Brunswick, along with the homes and properties of thousands who were living there. After he viewed the devastation, the lieutenant-governor of New Brunswick, George Stracey Smyth, claimed that the Aroostook and St. John valleys, with their rich stocks of lumber, were critical to the survival of the colony.

In an effort to resolve the dispute, the U.S. and Britain appointed separate commissioners to map the area. Not surprisingly, the commissioners were also unable to agree and eventually both claims were laid before William I, the king of the Netherlands, who had agreed to settle the dispute. The arguments for both sides were extensive and centred on everything from historical evidence to the definition of the Atlantic Ocean. The U.S. brief alone was reportedly 588 pages long, the British 418 pages. In 1831, William I selected the Saint John and St. Francis

CANADA UNDER ATTACK

rivers as the border between Nova Scotia and Maine. The effort was clearly a compromise and almost immediately accepted by Britain. The Maine legislature, under pressure from lumber interests, refused to ratify the decision. Once again the border was in dispute.

A few months after they rejected the border suggested by King William I, Maine was still determined to secure the territory it regarded as its own. Despite warnings from President Andrew Jackson that they should refrain from acting on their claim, the Maine Legislature decided to incorporate the village of Mada-waska, along with over 10,000 square kilometres of land in the disputed terri-tory. Elections were held in the village but some, including the French settlers, refrained from voting. Regardless, they held a town meeting attended by some 40 citizens and elected several town councillors before British officials arrived to disband the meeting. At another meeting encouraged by Maine officials, they met to choose a representative to the legislature. This time, the lieutenant-governor of New Brunswick became involved. He arrived in Madawaska with the New Bruns-wick attorney general, a local sheriff, and a complement of militia and promptly arrested four of the men who were most heavily involved with the Madawaska elections. Three of the four were fined $50 each and imprisoned for three months in a New Brunswick prison. In March 1832 the government of Maine accepted what amounted to a secret, million dollar bribe from Washington to refrain from pursuing their claim to the region. Washington intended to accept the recommen-dations of King William I but Maine withdrew from the secret pact and the Senate was forced to reject the arbitration.

Mutual frustration built on both sides of the border, along with the size of the troops massing there and within the disputed area. Settlers had no idea if they were American or British citizens. Also at issue were the hundreds of thousands of dollars worth of timber in the region, timber that was steadily growing in value as the dispute wore on. Dispatches were sent to both Washington and London, seek-ing support. The U.S. government was not anxious to launch another war with Britain and in Britain; Prime Minister Lord Palmerston considered the Aroostook problem to be little more than a nuisance.

Palmerston sent word that Britain would continue to exercise jurisdiction in the disputed area until a settlement could be reached. But a settlement seemed unlikely in that climate. Given the terms of union, the U.S. Senate was unlikely to approve a settlement that Maine did not support and Maine itself seemed to be quickly adopting a take-all or take-war approach. As a compromise, Palmerston suggested that each side appoint a commissioner to investigate the claims of both sides. They were further given instructions to survey the area and locate geographical features mentioned in the 1783 treaty. Suspecting that what Palmerston was really looking for was compromise rather than the truth, and not wishing to antagonize Maine, the U.S. government rejected Palmerston's suggestion.

Until they could negotiate a treaty the two sides agreed to create a virtual no man's land where no country claimed sovereignty. For a while the arrangement seemed to work and lumbermen from both sides arrived every winter to cull the forests. But in 1837 Congress passed a bill that would distribute proceeds from land sales to the states. Since the amount would be based on the state's population, Maine dispatched a land agent to produce an official census of the disputed region along the border in order to bolster their claim to the funds. The land agent, Rufus McIntyre, was a scrappy 70-year-old who was spoiling for a fight with the British. Reports filtered out that Mr. McIntyre was offering money to encourage settlement in the disputed area. But when McIntyre's men arrested a dozen so-called trespassers, including James McLaughlin, the New Brunswick appointed warden of the disputed territory, outrage overcame caution and the New Brunswickers were soon marching toward the valley. McLaughlin had already been transported to a prison in Bangor. At 1:00 a.m. on the night of February 12th, 40 armed men surrounded the house in which McIntyre and his companions slept. They arrested the men and McIntyre reportedly demanded to know by whose authority they were arresting him. "By this authority," the commander responded, brandishing his bayonet.[2] McIntyre and his companions were taken to Woodstock where a magistrate issued a warrant against them. They were then marched to a prison in Fredericton. Officials gamely offered to release the men if they agreed to quit the area. When McIntyre refused, the solicitor general of New Brunswick

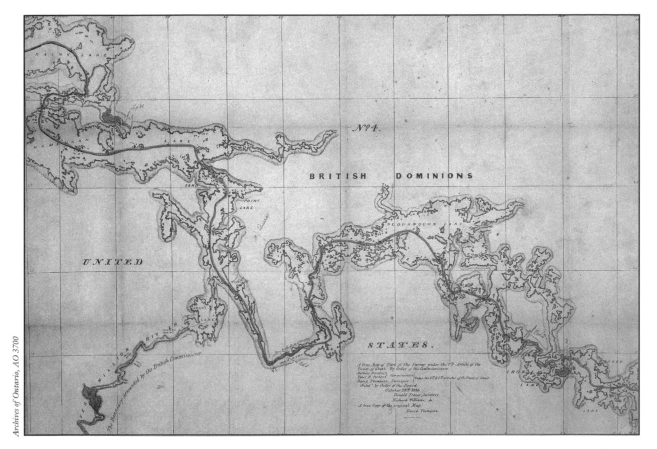

Archives of Ontario, AO 3700

assured him that he would supply him with a note that would explain that the man had no choice but to abandon his task or be imprisoned. Again he refused.

Outraged by this apparent attack on Maine's own soil, a posse was formed and immediately set off with the goal of rescuing McIntyre or taking revenge on the Canadians. By the middle of March, Maine had amassed over 2,000 troops in the Aroostook Valley. The legislature met and voted an additional 10,000 troops and approved $800,000 in funds for the defence of the state. New Brunswick also massed their troops along the border and ventured into the disputed territory. In response, Maine warned that if challenged its soldiers would not hesitate to retaliate.

A true map of the survey under the seventh article of the Treaty of Ghent by order of the commissioners, 1826.

In the midst of these escalating tensions, some more level-headed men released McIntyre, McLaughlin, and the other imprisoned men. But the newspapers on both sides of the border continued to whip up the populace. They condemned the arrests of citizens of their respective countries and suggested that the invasion of their cities was imminent. They celebrated their soldiers and extolled their citizens to be brave. "Let the sword by drawn and the scabbard be thrown away!" read the headlines of the *Kennebec Journal*. War seemed inevitable. In Upper Canada, Lieutenant-Governor Sir George Arthur declared, "I don't see how this can be ended without a general war." In the U.S., citizens were further riled to learn that an American had been tossed into a New Brunswick jail for whistling "Yankee Doodle" and told that he would not be released until he learned to whistle "God Save the Queen."

While the politicians postured and the soldiers rattled their sabres, the "war" began to take on an almost comical tone. One incident occurred when a group of American and Canadian lumbermen were drinking in the same tavern in apparent peace. When one mischievous soul raised his glass to toast Maine, a brawl broke out. According to local legend a pig that wandered in from Canada was shot, and one unfortunate Maine farmer's cow was taken hostage by the magistrate of Kent, New Brunswick — apparently it was later rescued by the Maine militia.

Inevitably, there was a darker side to the war. Soldiers would mysteriously disappear from their campsites and never return. A soldier by the name of Hiram T. Smith died, but no one is really sure how he succumbed. Explanations have ranged from being run over by a supply wagon to drowning in a local pond. Whatever the cause, a plaque was raised to mark the site of his death in the summer of 1839.

While the soldiers on both sides kept themselves busy building fortifications, the U.S. and British government's struggled to find a peaceful solution to the crisis. In the end, they appointed two men — Daniel Webster, a failed presidential candidate who had been given the post of secretary of state, and Alexander Baring, First Baron Ashburton. The two, who happened to be good friends, worked to find a solution that would be acceptable to all parties. For his part, Ashburton

CANADA UNDER ATTACK

refused to relinquish any territories north of the Saint John River. The dispute was finally settled in 1842. The United States received 18,000 square kilometres and the British received 12,950. The British agreed to pay the Americans reparations while the Americans agreed to pay the British for expenses they incurred while defending the area. Webster met the senate in a secret session in order to convince them to support the treaty. During that secret meeting he produced a map that he had said he had found in the Paris archives while researching records of the boundary. The map was purportedly marked by Benjamin Franklin and apparently entirely supported the British claims. Today, most historians believe the map to be a clever forgery created by Webster to sell the plan or by someone else sympathetic to the British cause.

The Aroostook War was really the war that wasn't. It is alternately known as the Lumberman's War, for the lumberman who made up most of the Maine militia, or the Pork n' Beans War, for the food the soldiers ate while they waited in their camps for the war to start. It was a war that the fledgling state of Maine was to be eager for, but that both Britain and Washington were determined to avoid.

CHAPTER NINE:
THE IRISH RAIDS

For over 20 years Canada's borders remained silent. Then the rumblings began. Throughout the winter of 1865 the good people of Campobello Island, the Nova Scotia colony, had listened to the rumours. A well-funded, well-organized, well-armed group of Irish American militants were hoping to pick a fight with the British. They were known as the Fenian Brotherhood and had been founded in 1859 in New York, as an offshoot of the Irish Republican Army. The two groups had a common goal — the liberation of Ireland — but they did not agree on the method. Some thought that an uprising in Ireland was the answer while others favoured an invasion of Canada as a way to get British attention. Most of the Fenians were battle-hardened veterans of the Civil War and most had found themselves unemployed when the war ended.

Fiercely loyal to Ireland and violently anti-English, the Fenians decided that if they could not launch an invasion and force the English from Ireland, they'd attempt the next best thing and force them from Canada. At worst, they hoped their fight would spark a wider conflict, pitting the entire United States against Britain. But what they most hoped for was to capture Canada and offer it in exchange for a free Ireland. By the time Campobello Island heard the rumours of an imminent invasion, the Fenians already had supplies in position along the border, generously provided by the demobilizing Union Army. All of Nova Scotia was a potential target. The colony was in the midst of a debate over Confederation and it was starting to look like voters would reject the idea altogether. The Fenians did not expect to meet much resistance. Campobello Island, isolated and sparsely populated, was at more risk than most and the people knew it. When a New Brunswick militia officer entered the general store to post a notice requesting new recruits, three patrons dropped their purchases and joined on the spot. By the time the Fenian sails were sighted, New Brunswick had 5,000 regulars, volunteers, and militia guarding its borders.

The military received intelligence, warning of an imminent attack, on St. Patrick's Day. Citizens were assigned to keep watch and the newly minted militia was mobilized. They waited but nothing happened. By the end of the month the rumours had quieted and everyone became anxious to get back to normal. The government disbanded the local militia and assured the people that all was well. It wasn't. By April 1866, 1,000 Fenians had gathered in Maine, directly across the water from Campobello Island. And more were on their way. Michael Murphy, a Fenian leader in Toronto, was ordered to bring a contingent of his men to the Maine–New Brunswick border, but the telegram was intercepted by Canadian officials and Murphy and several companions were arrested on a train in Cornwall, Ontario. A substantial cache of cash, weapons, and ammunition was captured with Murphy. Murphy and his companions were jailed on charges of treason until they escaped and took refuge in New York City. News of the capture arrived alongside the news that the Fenians were gathering. In New Brunswick, the volunteers quickly mustered and two British ships were dispatched to wait out the conflict in the bay.

On April 17, the U.S. Navy boarded the *Ocean Spray* — a former Confederate ship that the Fenians had taken command of — took charge of the 500 rifles the ship carried, and warned the crew that that U.S. neutrality would be strictly enforced. The Fenians, confronted by an annoyed American government and facing a clear, strong resistance from the Canadians, delayed their plans to attack. The delay did not last long. In Niagara the Canadians had also received warning of an attack, but there was little they could do except wait. Attacking the Irish could be perceived as an attack on the Americans, something everyone wanted to avoid. As the sun skirted the edge of the horizon on the morning of June 1st, the sleepy residents of Fort Erie awakened to see a flotilla of ships sailing toward them. The masts bore a strange flag, a harp and crown on a field of green. On that cool, clear morning, a formidable force of nearly 1,000 Fenians slipped unhindered into their boats and rowed quietly across the Niagara River, pulling

A Group of Fenian Volunteers, 1865.

ashore at what is now the intersection of Bowen Road and Niagara Boulevard. They carried extra uniforms and arms with them for the flood of new recruits they expected to join them. They had come, they informed the local populace, to free them from the yoke of British tyranny.

When no Canadians responded to what they viewed as an insane call to arms, the Fenians were astounded. What was wrong with these people? Did they not realize that liberty was within their grasp?

The Irishman Doran Killian had a plan to seize the island of Campobello Island. His theory was that the occupation would keep the British troops from being sent back to Ireland, where the real revolution would take place. The American government did nothing to stop them — they were not willing to risk war with the Canadians, but they were not above allowing the Fenians to cause the Canadians and the British a few problems. After all, the Canadians seemed to have been a little too helpful to the Confederate armies.

THE IRISH RAIDS

For their part, the Canadians were more exasperated than afraid and certainly more annoyed with the Fenians than eager to join them. On Campobello Island the Irishmen ate a leisurely lunch provided by the locals — who were no doubt hopeful that if they fed this crazed bunch of marauders they would move on. Instead, the Canadians watched in fascinated horror as the Irishmen stretched out in the shade beneath a stand of maples to take a nap. But when the small group of invaders realized that expected reinforcements would not be arriving, they eventually left. To the Canadians it must have appeared that the Fenians were engaged in more of a social enterprise than a military one. Events would soon prove them wrong.

Undeterred by their failed raids on Fort Erie and Campobello Island, the Fenians turned their attention to Niagara. By May 22, 1866, almost 1,000 Fenian troops, led by Colonel John O'Neill and Colonel Owen Star, had massed in Buffalo, New York. While the Fenians were successful recruiters and fundraisers their successes made avoiding the attention of authorities almost impossible. British operatives easily infiltrated Irish American communities and knew every move the Fenians made. They made sure that the Canadian authorities knew too. Across the river, the Fenians quietly reported to their commanders and were then dispersed in smaller groups to the homes of local Irish Americans. At midnight on June 1, Colonel Starr rowed quietly across the Niagara River and quickly secured a landing point for troops at the Village of Bertie Township. O'Neill followed a few hours later with the rest of the troops. The plan was to take the Welland Canal, thereby cutting off the vital shipping route between Lakes Erie and Ontario.

By 9:00 a.m. two columns of troops marched beneath a bright green banner toward Fort Erie and the local rail yard. They were a motley bunch. Some wore "peculiar green jackets,"[1] others United States Army uniforms, but for the most part there was "nothing to distinguish them from an ordinary gathering of about one thousand men."[2] O'Neill took a small group and headed for the local rail yard. A loaded locomotive had just pulled out of the station and a couple of the more adventurous men jumped onto a handcar to pursue the train. After burning down a bridge they gave up and rejoined the main group who had set up camp at Thomas Newbeggin's farm. At first, they met no immediate opposition and they did not attract the Irish Canadian recruits they hoped for. The extra 1,000 muskets they had brought to arm the recruits lay piled in a corner of the camp.

While 14,000 Canadian militia had been called up when the Fenians began to gather in Buffalo, only a handful were actually ready for service when O'Neill and his men arrived. The Canadians realized that the likely target was the Welland Canal and the rail line that ran parallel to it so troops were stationed at both the south and north ends of the canal: Port Colborne and St. Catharines. At Port Colborne that included 800 men, primarily young, eager college students from Toronto. They lacked heavy weapons and logistical support and were commanded by Lieutenant-Colonel Alfred Booker, a Hamilton businessman with very little military experience. Booker received orders to join his forces to the regiments of more experienced British regulars under the command of Colonel George Peacock stationed in St. Catharines. Early on the morning of June 2, Booker's men boarded rail cars that would take them to Ridgeway. From there they would march to Stephensville to meet Peacock and his men.

O'Neill had his own spies in the Canadian and British camps and he knew he would stand little chance against the combined numbers of Peacock and Booker's. His only option was to attack Booker before he reached Stephensville. So while Booker was loading his men onto railcars, O'Neill gave orders to several regiments of his Irish Republican Army (IRA) to launch an overnight march to Ridgeway. By the early morning hours of June 2 they had taken up position on Limestone Ridge just north of Ridgeway. Colonel Booker and his boxcars full of soldiers arrived at Ridgeway, where several local farmers informed him that the Fenians were already there. Inexplicably, Booker ignored that information and at 6:00 a.m. he ordered his men to begin their march along Ridge Road toward Stephensville. The men moved forward but were forced to leave their reserve ammunition behind when it became clear that no transportation had been arranged for it. They had not gone far when two Canadian detectives arrived to inform them that the Fenians had fallen in behind them. Almost simultaneously they heard the sound of rifle fire. Booker immediately ordered his men to take cover and return fire. He expected Peacock to arrive soon. Peacock had received reinforcements during the night and they refused to budge until they finished their breakfast. Peacock had no idea that Booker's troops were already under fire. Luckily, it appeared that Booker's young Canadians did not need any help from the British regulars.

As Peacock's reinforcements were eating their breakfast, Booker's Canadians were already pressing the Fenian line. They had advanced almost a half mile after barely an hour. Then tragedy struck. Some of the Canadian front line spied horses in the woods and shouted warning of a Fenian cavalry advance. The inexperienced Booker did not hesitate and immediately called for his cavalry unit to gather in a square formation. They made a perfect target, which the Fenians immediately took advantage of. Seeing his men fall and realizing there was no impending cavalry attack, Booker called them off. But it was too late. Falling back they encountered one of the reserve companies who, believing a general retreat was being called, broke into a panicked run. The Fenians, who had been close to calling a retreat of their own, took full advantage of the perfect target that the Canadians presented on the road below as they ran down their path with their rifles tucked under their arms. Then they filled in behind the Canadians to pursue the retreat, pausing to gather a few souvenirs from the battlefield. The pitched battles continued to Ridgeway, where the Fenians suddenly turned and headed toward Fort Erie. The Canadians had suffered nine killed, 36 wounded, and six taken prisoner.[3]

Almost at the same time, a tiny tugboat made its way up the Welland Canal and landed men from the Dunville and Welland militias near Fort Erie. These Canadian troops were tasked with rounding up any Fenian strays they could find. It worked well until the main body of the Fenian Army arrived and began to engage them. The Dunville militia jumped back on the tugboat but the Welland militia kept up a spirited and bloody fight. Before the rifle fire finally ended, six Canadians were wounded and a further 36 had been taken prisoner. The Fenians suffered nine killed and 14 wounded.

At Fort Erie, O'Neill took quick stock of the situation. None of his own expected reinforcements had arrived and newly arrived scouts informed him that Canadian and British reinforcements would get there at any time. O'Neill decided to pull his men back to Buffalo. The orderly retreat turned into a melee as the

Irishmen realized that there were too few boats. Worried that their last day on earth might be spent on Canadian soil, some of the Fenians leapt into the river and tried to swim to the American side; others paddled across on logs and makeshift rafts. Those who made their way onto boats were boarded once they reached the middle of the river their ships and arrested by member of the United States Navy.

The battle of Ridgeway was over but the Fenian raids were not. On June 7, between 500 and 1,000[4] Fenian brethren crossed the Vermont-Quebec border under the leadership of West Point graduate Brigadier General Samuel Spear. Appearing and acting more like a mob, this group advanced 10 kilometres into Canada and planted their bright green flag. They met no initial resistance because the Canadian militia had fallen back in the face of a much larger group of invaders. Instead, they plundered local farms and villages, stole chickens, pigs, and liquor, and antagonized the local population. On June 5, President Andrew Jackson declared that the U.S. Neutrality Laws of 1818 would be enforced. The Fenians were furious at what they considered a betrayal by their own government. When Spear heard that Canadian reinforcements would arrive at any moment and that the U.S. government had impounded his stores of ammunition and supplies in Vermont, he called a retreat and the Fenian Army fled for the border.

The Canadian militia caught up with one group of retreating Fenians near Pigeon Hill. They charged over the Fenian defences with their sabres drawn. The startled Fenians broke into a run for the border but 16 of them were taken prisoner during the brief battle. The border was finally quiet, but Canada had not seen the last of the Fenians. While the Canadian militia were welcomed as heroes in their home communities, John O'Neill and many of his Fenians were receiving the same hero's welcome in Irish American communities. Many of those arrested in Canada were given death sentences that were later commuted to lengthy prison sentences. Those arrested by U.S. authorities were quietly released once it seemed clear that the border would remain quiet. Canadians were incensed. While the army attempted to enforce neutrality laws, the U.S. government had clearly been content to look the other way when the Fenians had launched attacks on Canadian targets and they certainly were not taking the raids seriously now that they were over.

St. Alban's Raid

Occasionally, Canada also served as a launching site for attacks on the United States. As a neutral player in the American Civil War, Canada became a favourite destination for Confederate prisoners escaping from northern Union prisons. Bennett Young was one of those prisoners who took refuge in Quebec. But Young was also a fervent believer in the southern cause and he was not content to simply save himself. He was determined to find a way to aid the Confederate cause from his position in Canada.

He hatched a plan that he hoped would both supply much needed funds to the depleted Confederate treasury and force the Union to deploy troops away from the current battlefields to the relatively undefended northern territories. He slipped back across the border in the fall of 1864 to pitch his plan to his superiors in the Confederate Army. They quickly agreed to provide him with the necessary funds and he once again made his way into Canada.

On October 10, 1864, he crossed the border with two compatriots and the tiny group made their way to the village of St. Alban's, Vermont. They checked into a local hotel and informed the desk clerk that they were from St. John's and had come down for a sporting holiday. For the next two weeks small groups of "Canadians" arrived to join Young's group until finally there were 21 (an entire platoon). The morning of October 29, Young climbed onto the hotel steps and loudly declared that St. Albans was the property of the Confederacy. While several of his platoon rounded up the terrified villagers on the village green, the rest robbed three of the local banks. With over $200,000 stuffed in their saddlebags, the entire group galloped toward the Canadian border on stolen horses. They had planned to set the entire town ablaze but their homemade bombs failed and a single shed was the only building that burned.

As a victorious Young galloped into Quebec, he and his men were promptly arrested by Canadian authorities. Despite demands from the American government, the Canadians declared the St. Alban's Raid to be an act of war and refused to turn over Young or any of his followers. They did, however, eventually return most of the money.

The raids had gained the Fenians nothing. They had not sparked fresh American-British hostilities nor had they significantly aided the efforts of the Irish Republican Army in Ireland. In fact, the insurrection there was largely finished by 1867. However, the conflict did have a lasting effect on Canada. Those first raids on Campobello Island revitalized the cause of Confederation in the Maritimes and helped bring a previously reluctant New Brunswick into the Dominion of Canada. Ridgeway and the other battles fought by the Canadian militia also helped give birth to a new-found Canadian nationalism and pride just as the Dominion of Canada was created. It also provided the impetus for the creation of a permanent Canadian militia and one of the new Canadian government's first acts was to create a standing militia of over 40,000 men.

Across the border, the Fenians were still alive and well, but although O'Neill

The Fenians at their Pigeon Hill Camp. May 25, 1870.

had received considerable credit for the Canadian operations, there was dissention among his political allies. By 1870, O'Neill became convinced that in order to save the Fenian cause, and perhaps his own political future, he must once again invade Canada. He was able to lay a massive store of arms and munitions — 15,000 weapons and three million rounds of ammunition — in his base at Franklin, Vermont. His call for volunteers was less successful — just 400 Fenians would agree to invade Canada again.

Undeterred, O'Neill crossed the border with his 400 well armed men on May 25, 1870. Already waiting for him was the local Canadian militia, many of whom were farmers who had lost property during the first Fenian raids on the Missisquoi in 1866. At noon, U.S. Marshal General Foster rode up to the Canadian lines at Eccles Hill to assure the Canadians that the U.S. intended to enforce neutrality laws and that they would act as soon as possible. In the meantime, he had also brought a message from General O'Neill, who wished to assure the Canadians that the Fenians would conduct their battle in a civilized manner: women and children would be safe and looting would be prohibited. The Canadian commander, Lieutenant-Colonel Brown Chamberlin, stared down the American marshal and replied that he would receive no messages from pirates and marauders. His men were fighting in defence of their homes and country; they would take no comfort in knowing that additional atrocities would not be committed against their families.

Foster left the Canadian encampment just as the Fenian main guard was sighted, their column moving at double pace down the narrow path. The Canadian troops, well hidden in the bush and buildings, began to fire just as the first group came within range. The surprised Fenians immediately broke ranks and took cover wherever they could find it. General O'Neill hurried to a brick farmhouse close to the Vermont border, where he continued to direct the Fenian effort. His men had brought a field gun with them and he ordered it brought to the front. Before it could be fired the Canadian commander called on his men to charge the Fenian line. Once again the Irishmen scattered. The owner of the farmhouse where O'Neill had taken refuge ordered him out and almost immediately Marshal Foster arrived with his deputies to place the Fenian general under arrest. They placed him in a covered carriage and raced back to the Vermont border. With their general gone and faced with a fierce Canadian opposition, the rest of O'Neill's troops broke into a wild dash for the border. Two days later, the Fenians attempted another raid near Holbrook Corners, Quebec, but they were quickly turned back by a large force of Canadian militia and British regulars. At Buffalo, Detroit, and Ogdensburg, Fenians who had gathered to invade Canada heard the news of the defeats of their brethren and the arrests of O'Neill and immediately abandoned any thought of continuing their assault on Canada.

The Fenian raids in Ontario and Quebec were over. O'Neill received a sentence of six months in a U.S. jail. The Fenian organization was in disarray but shortly after his release in 1870, O'Neill was once again plotting to invade Canada. That time his intended target was Manitoba. He scraped together a few of the armaments and ammunition that had not be taken by U.S. authorities and managed to gather an additional 40 men. Although it was a far cry from the 1,000 he originally had, O'Neill thought he would have assistance from Métis leader Louis Riel and his men, who were already engaged in open rebellion against the Canadian government. Unfortunately for O'Neill, he was arrested as soon as he crossed the border by the U.S. authorities who had, by that time, had enough of the Fenians. They were marched back across the border, their weapons were confiscated, and they were thrown in U.S. jails.

General O'Neill's career was over, his cause effectively dead. He died a broken man. Members of the Fenian movement would continue to agitate in Canada, particularly in the Northwest, where they actively recruited members, but no additional raids were launched. The lasting legacy of the great cause of Irish nationalism was the birth of Canadian nationalism and the baptism, through fire and blood, of the Canadian military.

CHAPTER TEN:
THE PHANTOM INVASION

Count Max Lynar Louden was many things. He was a charming, debonair member of Europe's displaced nobility. He was a man of German origin living in America at a time when America was at war with Germany. He was also a convicted bigamist.

When Louden stood up and accepted his sentence for bigamy in a New York City courtroom, he made a request. He needed to speak to the assistant district attorney who had prosecuted him. He had a story to tell, and if he was about to go to jail he needed to clear his conscience first.

Louden's story was an incredible one, even in a time of war when rumours abounded and everyone was on high alert. He was, he confessed, the head of a secret German plot to invade Canada from the United States. A very well-funded plot: Louden claimed that he had access to well over 16 million dollars.

Almost immediately after Canada declared war on Germany on August 4, 1914, rumours had spread that a German invasion from the United States was imminent. Those rumours had been fuelled by the German propaganda machine, which hoped to unsettle the Canadian public and possibly force their withdrawal from the conflict in Europe. Louden's plot, he revealed, had been in place since October 1914, soon after the war began. It relied on the co-operation of 150,000 German reservists who were living freely in the United States, waiting to be called to duty for the motherland. Louden had at his command an entire army corps as well as two regiments of artillery and one of sharpshooters. All were lying in wait close to the border, in secret "centres" set up in Philadelphia, New York, Boston, and Detroit. At a moment's notice they were ready to have the entire army at the Canadian border within 10 days.

Louden had also devised a plan to explain the presence of so many Germans along the border. They would use the cover of German singing societies gathered to participate in a *Saengerfest*. If they had to they would sing, for as Louden eloquently pointed out: a German could sing as well as he could shoot. Louden assured his audience that arming his force was not a problem. American arms manufacturers would sell to anyone, providing they had the money to pay for the goods. He could provide arms for a million men within a few days if he was given the money to pay for it.

The simplest part of the plan was the invasion itself. It would, he argued, be over in less than 24 hours. The German troops would land at six critical points along the Canadian border, capturing each and taking out any lines of communication that could be used by the Canadian Army. The Welland Canal would be completely destroyed. The Canadian forces would be surrounded and, if necessary, annihilated. Louden would lead the fifth troop to Ottawa himself.

The American military dismissed Louden's claims as a last-ditch fantastical claim by a man facing serious jail time. But the newspapers on both sides of the border ran with the story. For a few days, while the story circulated, the public was on high alert looking for potential conspirators and secret German reservists. Eventually, with no sign of any imminent invasion, the story faded away.

The invasion plans did not.

In the fall of 1914 a small package was delivered to one of Germany's chief intelligence officers — Captain Franz von Papen. The return address on the package seemed innocuous enough — Eden Bower Farm, Oregon. Inside the package were detailed plans for the invasion of Canada. Its author was a German agent operating under the guise of an Oregon farmer. His plan outlined an invasion of Canada using powerboats and machine guns. His targets were the major ports along the U.S.-Canada border; his goal was to keep Canadian troops from aiding the British.

The plan was eventually given to Count Johann Heinrich Graf von Bernstorff, the German ambassador to the United States. Although it was not revealed until well after the war ended, von Bernstorff was heavily involved in planning and recruiting for the German war effort in North America. He also had access to a huge fund of cash for use in his efforts. For most of the war, von Bernstorff and other German operatives spent enormous sums on the recruitment of pro-German saboteurs and on funding their sabotage efforts.

Von Bernstorff gave the invasion plan serious consideration along with two other proposals for an invasion, including one that would go through British Columbia and would have involved German reservists in the United States supported by German warships from the Pacific theatre. In 1914, von Bernstorff offered up an alternative plan that called for the bombing of the Welland Canal. The canal, which offered the only route around Niagara Falls and served as a main artery for both exports and imports, was of supreme economic importance to Canada. More important to the German operatives was the psychological effect that its destruction would have on the Canadian people. For good measure they included plans to destroy the railway terminals in southern Ontario and the grain elevators that surrounded Toronto.

British intelligence officers learned of the plot against the Welland Canal and quickly informed the Canadians, who deployed no less than 1,000 men and women around the canal under various guises. When von Papen realized that the area was too well defended to attack, he suspended the plan.

The majority of the plots and attempts at sabotage were launched from the United States, which remained neutral for most of the First World War. Sharing a largely undefended and open border, Canada was particularly vulnerable to operatives entering from the U.S. Canada had not yet developed a spy or anti-terrorism agency so they relied on the leadership of Lieutenant-Colonel Percy Sherwood, head of the Dominion Police. In turn, Sherwood relied on a complicated, somewhat informal network of telegraph operators, customs and immigration officers, special police, military personnel, private investigators, and watchmen. He developed a close relationship with the Pinkertons, the legendary U.S. private investigation firm. Despite a somewhat rocky relationship, during which the U.S. government accused the Pinkertons of playing both sides, they helped maintain Canada's defence for much of the war.

On December 12, 1914, Japan joined Canada in the war against Germany and the German government suspected that Japanese reinforcements would be sent to Europe via Canada's Pacific coast and then through the country's extensive rail network. In December 1914, the German Foreign Office sent von Bernstoff orders to disrupt, by any means possible, any potential routes for troop movements. A secret telegram from the German Foreign Office warned, "The transportation of Japanese troops through Canada must be prevented at all costs if necessary by blowing up Canadian railways. It would probably be advisable to employ Irish for this purpose in the first instance as it is almost impossible for Germans to enter Canada. You should discuss the matter with the Military Attache. The strictest secrecy is indispensable."[1]

The most obvious target was the Canadian Pacific Railway (CPR). Von Bernstoff directed von Papen to lead the operation. He in turn contacted a German reserve officer living in Guatemala, Werner von Horn, and contracted the job of bombing the CPR lines to him. Von Papen wrote von Horn a $700 cheque for his services.

Again the Canadians received some warning, but von Horn was still able to detonate a bomb on the CPR bridge over the St. Croix River between New Brunswick and Maine. The bomb did little damage and caused a mere six hour delay. There were suspicions but no one was really sure who had led the sabotage efforts. Canada did not get solid proof of von Papen and von Horn's involvement in the plot until much later, when von Papen allowed British authorities to search his luggage and seize his chequebook. Von Horn was eventually extradited to Canada and served time in a New Brunswick prison.

While von Horn fought his extradition, von Papen searched for another operative to launch attacks on targets in Canada. He recruited close to 100 German sympathizers to act as shock troops in the event of a German invasion of Canada. Additional attempts on the CPR lines were reportedly planned. A bridge bombing in Quebec was foiled by bad weather, and plans for another attack between Andover and Perth fizzled. Von Papen also recruited George Fuchs, a relative of Paul Koenig, one of von Papen's agents, and paid him $18 per week to monitor traffic on the Welland Canal with an eye to launching another strategic attack there. Fuchs was unemployed and an alcoholic, expendable in the German's eyes, but certainly not reliable. The original plans called for Fuchs to row across the canal and deliver a boatload of explosives to German operatives in Canada. Fuchs got into a fight and was arrested by the police. As he was being questioned, he mentioned Koenig's name and police decided to search his apartment. Unfortunately for von Papen and von Horn, Koenig had kept extensive records of his involvement, and theirs, in nearly every sabotage effort in North America. These records proved invaluable when von Papen was indicted by the Americans in April 1916, on a charge of plotting to blow-up the Welland Canal. Unfortunately, by that time von Papen was already feeling the heat and had made his escape to Germany.

Reports of German activities in and around Canada had reached near hysterical proportions by the middle of the war. British authorities were particularly vigilant about reporting every rumour, substantiated or not. Sir Courtenay Bennett, the British consul-general in New York City, was one of the most vigilant. He repeatedly warned of an impending German attack on Canada. Large numbers of well-armed Germans were massing on the border, he reported, and by 1915 their numbers had exceeded 80,000. Lieutenant-Colonel Sherwood of the Dominion Police dismissed Bennett's claims and Canadian, British, and American agencies disproved many others. While there were a minimum of nine incidents of violent sabotage in Canada between 1914 and 1915, there many discovered "plots" that simply did not exist and proved embarrassing to both government officials and the innocent "conspirators."

There was nothing innocent about several conspirators, who by 1915 had turned their attention to the city of Windsor, Ontario. Albert Carl Kaltschmidt was one of von Papen's earliest recruits. In May 1915, Kaltschmidt, a machine shop owner from Detroit, recruited Charles Francis Respa and his brother-in-law, Charles Schmidt. It was clear that Kaltschmidt's loyalties did not lie with the United States, where he had settled, but remained with Germany. "We must do something for our dear Fatherland," he told Respa and Schmidt. "You should not care anything for America or Americans because America will throw you out from your work, but we will give you good jobs after the war is over, and Americans will trample you with their feet."[2]

Respa's motivations were not purely nationalistic. Apparently he had not completed his military service in Germany and faced arrest there if he returned, which he desperately wanted to do. Kaltschmidt suggested that providing assistance to the fatherland in North America, by way of espionage or sabotage, might free him from this obligation and ease his return to Germany. Schmidt became involved simply by being married to Respa's sister.

Kaltschmidt considered targets in Detroit before dismissing them as too well guarded. He briefly considered attaching dynamite to a passenger train as it passed through a tunnel near the St. Clair River. He also sent Respa and other operatives to gauge the vulnerability of rail lines near Winnipeg. Eventually he turned his attention to the Peabody Overall Factory across the Detroit River in Walkerville (Windsor), Ontario, and to the Windsor Armoury. The factory supplied uniforms, gloves, and clothing to the British Army and the armoury trained and housed Canadian soldiers and served as a warehouse for Canadian military equipment. The factory was a particularly tempting target since Kaltschmidt had an existing relationship with its night watchman, a man by the name of William Lefler.

On June 21, 1915, Kaltschmidt met with Respa and Lefler and offered them $200 each to bomb the factory and the armoury. Kaltschmidt had come prepared. Once the men had agreed to his plan, he gave them two timer devices and 156 sticks of dynamite. That night Respa and his sister, Mrs. Schmidt, boarded a ferry and carried the dynamite, packed in their luggage, across the border. Respa hurried to the Peabody Factory where he handed one of the timers and half of the dynamite to Lefler and the hurried to the Armoury where he planted the other half of the dynamite at to the rear, where the Canadian Army barracks were, and set the timer. He and Mrs. Schmidt then hurried back to the ferry and crossed over to Detroit. At 3:00 a.m. an explosion rocked the city of Windsor — the bomb at the Peabody Factory had gone off. The one at the armoury failed to ignite and was soon discovered by the authorities.

Canadian authorities immediately focused their investigation on the night watchman, Lefler. He was soon arrested. Lefler immediately gave up Respa and Schmidt as his co-conspirators. Respa was able to flee Detroit just before he was arrested but he quickly ran out of money and returned. Authorities promptly arrested him and he quickly confessed and handed over information on Kaltschmidt, who was put under surveillance by the Pinkertons. But U.S. authorities failed to arrest Kaltschmidt and Canada was unable to extradite him. Kaltschmidt confidently continued to finance clandestine activities. When the U.S. finally entered the war, Kaltschmidt's luck ran out. Thanks to the dossier compiled by the Pinkertons,[3] he was arrested and charged with making explosive devices intended to blow-up factories in Canada, and with plotting to dynamite the Grand Trunk Railway between Port Huron and Sarnia. During the trial it was revealed that Kaltschmidt had received $70,000[4] from the German embassy to finance his activities.

During Kaltschmidt's trial a munitions factory in the tiny town of Nobel, Ontario, exploded. Several explosions occurred simultaneously, making it unlikely that they were the result of an accident. The military was immediately called to investigate and newspapers were filled with the accounts of possible German sabotage. The Pinkertons were called in and focused their efforts on determining which of the factory's employees were of German or Austrian descent. The Pinkerton agent working the case developed a list of men of German descent whom he considered to be possible suspects. The men, on nothing more than the Pinkerton agent's hunch, were immediately fired, though they were never charged.

In February 1916 a massive fire broke out on Parliament Hill in Ottawa, taking the lives of seven people. The papers were filled with accounts of the fire and speculation about the involvement of German operatives. Several men were questioned but no one was charged. A report released in May 1916 concluded that there was no clear evidence that the fire had been deliberately set. That did not seem to matter to the public at large. Their imaginations had been caught. The country was rife with German operatives.

With the Ontario border heavily scrutinized and Canadian civilians, military, and government employees on the watch for suspicious activity, German operatives decided to turn their attention to the west. Franz Bopp, the German consul general in San Francisco, was tasked with leading the sabotage operations in the west. Like von Papen he was provided with ample funds by the German foreign office. In April 1915, Vice Consul Wilhelm von Brincken, one of Bopp's assistants, met with a man named von Koolbergen, a Dutchman and naturalized British citizen. Von Koolbergen was offered $100 for the use of his passport, to which he readily agreed. The conversation continued and finally Bopp's emissaries offered von Koolbergen $3,000 to blow-up the Canadian Pacific Railway tunnel between Revelstoke and Vancouver. Von Koolbergen agreed and then left the German operatives.

Whether he had been leading the operatives on from the beginning or had simply experienced cold feet, von Koolbergen immediately contacted the British consulate and confessed the entire plot and von Brincken's involvement. The Canadian authorities, working with CP Rail, concocted a plan whereby von Koolbergen could collect his money and provide evidence that would help them convict von Brincken and other German operatives. Von Koolbergen crossed the border into Canada as planned and a few days later Vancouver newspapers carried a story about the collapse of a railway tunnel in the mountains between Vancouver and Revelstoke. Von Koolbergen returned to San Francisco to collect his money from the Germans. Von Brincken delightedly paid him $200 and asked him to return the following day for the balance of his fee.

After a series of secret meetings complete with secret passwords, skepticism, arguments, and threats of blackmail, von Brincken finally agreed to pay the crafty von Koolbergen $1,500. Von Koolbergen promptly disappeared with his winnings and without having committed any punishable crime. The Canadians were left without their evidence.

German espionage and sabotage in Canada died off once the United States entered the war and German operatives no longer had a safe haven south of the border. But the extent of the German effort in Canada during the First World War was astounding. In addition to sabotage efforts against rail lines, canals, factories, and military targets, they recruited hundreds of operatives in Canada, including those from the Irish Canadian and Canadian Sikh communities, whom they supported in their fight for independence from Britain.

CHAPTER ELEVEN:
U-BOATS IN THE ST. LAWRENCE

May 11, 1942, dawned bright and clear and the people of Gaspé, Quebec, went about their business in much the same way that they always did. There was a war in progress — many of the people in this region had sons, brothers, and fathers fighting overseas — but the war itself seemed far away and less immediate than the commonplace tasks of everyday life.

The weather held throughout the evening. A half moon rose over the bay, casting it in a soft, bluish glow. The tide lapped gently along the shore. A few hours after midnight the dulled sounds of a distant explosion were heard. Then a much larger, much closer crash. Finally, the sky lit up with the lights of what seemed like a thousand fires. A few hours later another boom shook the coast and the glare of yet another fire coloured the horizon.

The war had come to Canada.

A mere 13 kilometres from shore a German U-boat had sunk a British banana boat commissioned to carry war supplies. Boats rushed out to rescue the survivors but it was too late for six unlucky sailors. Just as the exhausted survivors stepped onto shore, the second explosion lit the sky. The Dutch freighter *Leto*, leased by the British Ministry of War, was hit. Passing ships picked up what survivors they could find clinging to the wreckage and small rafts. The U-boat had struck so quickly and with such precision that the men of the *Leto* only had time to launch a single, small boat. A dozen seamen lost their lives.

The attacks shocked Canadians. Knowing that U-boats were busy in the St. Lawrence was one thing, actually being forced to witness an attack was quite another.

Until 1942 there had been no definitive German plan to attack in North American waters. The few U-boat attacks that had occurred in Canadian waters, particularly in the St. Lawrence, were considered to be accidents of chance or opportunity. In fact, U-boat crews attained a sort of mythical status in Canada. Tales abounded of U-boat captains arriving in villages to buy their groceries, have a beer in the local tavern, or enjoy a dance with a pretty girl in a local dance hall. Far from being a threatening element, the U-boats almost seemed romantic. All of that changed after the Japanese attacks on Pearl Harbour. Germany was officially at war with the United States and all of the previous restrictions placed on U-boat commanders by a German High Command eager to avoid antagonizing the Americans were abandoned. A flotilla of five large U-boats was dispatched to Canadian waters. Operation Drumbeat had begun.

With the majority of Canada's few naval vessels engaged elsewhere, only a minesweeper, two motor launches, and a small yacht remained to protect the entrance to the St. Lawrence. The area was considered to be a secondary target by both the Germans and the Allies and therefore of secondary importance for defence. Even Operation Drumbeat was meant to be a lightning strike rather than a sustained action. It turned out to be a devastating action that more closely resembled a prolonged storm. The combination of freshwater from the river, saltwater from the ocean, and rapidly fluctuating temperatures wreaked havoc on sonar equipment in the gulf. The area's notorious fogs helped hide the U-boats when they broke the surface. By the end of October, U-boats had sunk 19 merchant ships and two naval escorts.

The most devastating attack was yet to come. The *Caribou* had ferried citizens between Sydney, Nova Scotia, and Port-aux-Basques, Newfoundland, for years. On the morning of October 14th it was torpedoed by a German U-boat, a mere 60 kilometres from its destination. The ferry went down so quickly that only one lifeboat could be launched. The crew valiantly urged people into the lifeboat and when that was full they helped them on to pieces of debris and makeshift rafts. Other crew members lead disoriented, panicked passengers away from the sinking hull of the ship. When the last survivors were finally rescued they learned that only 15 of the 48 crew members had survived.

Many of the crew had gone down with the ship, others helping to save as many as they could before they were forced to abandon ship. Despite the crew's heroic efforts, the numbers were grim. Of the 237 souls who had set sail for Newfoundland that morning just over 100 survived. The loss of the *Caribou* ripped the heart out of Newfoundland. There were five pairs of brothers amongst the crew and several fathers and sons. Most were lost. Also lost was the Canadian sense of distance from the war, which had seemed so far away. The death and devastation that had, until then, been confined to a distant land had come home to Canada.

In August, U-boats launched attacks against ships in harbours in Labrador and Newfoundland, and against a convoy in the Straight of Belle Isle. The continued U-boat attacks fuelled a bitter debate over conscription in the Canadian Parliament and damaged the already fragile relationship between Quebec and the federal government. Quebec members of Parliament were furious over the seemingly inability of the government to protect their coastal constituencies. The Royal Canadian Air Force frequently tracked the U-boats but just as frequently lost them in the fog or was grounded by the mercurial Maritime weather. The quick moving U-boats frequently attacked before the ships were able to gather into the safety of a convoy. In September, *U-517* entered the St. Lawrence River, was almost immediately detected, and came under heavy fire from the RCAF. It was still able to escape and sink nine ships. By October 1942, U-boats had penetrated as far upriver as Rimouski, Quebec, just 300 kilometres from Quebec City.

The Germans did not stay long in the St. Lawrence. Instead they turned their attention to targets that were more lucrative and easily attacked. Military authorities had long expected an attack on highly exposed Bell Island. Its harbour was frequented by large ships and the iron ore mined there was in high demand from the various war machines. Early in the war the Canadian government had agreed to furnish Bell Island with several large guns and searchlights to aid in the defence of the harbour. The Newfoundland government recruited a militia, the Canadians provided training for the men, and the iron ore companies provided the barracks to house them. Air Raid Patrol wardens patrolled the island's streets to ensure that lights were doused and curtains drawn during blackouts.

On September 5, 1942, the harbour was full of ships. The *Saganaga* and the *Lord Strathcona*, each with their holds filled with iron ore, waited for a convoy to

Damage to the Scotia Pier caused by a torpedo fired by the German submarine U-518 on November 2, 1942. Taken on Bell Island, Newfoundland, November 3, 1942.

escort them to Nova Scotia. The *Evelyn B* was loaded with coal and waiting to unload. Numerous other ships — the *PLM 27*, *Rose Castle*, and *Drake-pool* among them — were busily exchanging the goods they had delivered to Bell Island for loads of iron ore. On the *Lord Strathcona*, Chief Engineer William Henderson watched as a torpedo tore through the calm waters of the harbour and slammed into the *Saganaga*. He checked his watch. It was

CANADA UNDER ATTACK

11:07 a.m. Less than three seconds later, "a second torpedo literally blew the *Saganaga* to pieces. Debris and iron ore was thrown up about 300 feet and, before the last of it had fallen back into the water, the *Saganaga* had disappeared."[1] Henderson immediately ordered his crew to their lifeboats and at 11:30 a.m. as the men of the *Lord Strathcona* were still attempting to rescue the men of their sister ship, the *Saganaga*, another torpedo slammed into the *Lord Strathcona*. A second torpedo slammed into the ship and it sank less than a minute and a half later. The crew of the *Evelyn B* immediately opened fire into the water where the torpedo had first appeared and is credited with driving off the U-boat, which was still lying in wait. The militia joined the fight from the battery and trained the heavy guns on the water. *U-513* suddenly broke the surface and raced to the safety of the open ocean.

The first battle of Bell Island was over. The second would begin just a few months later. On the night of November 2, 1942 *U-513*'s sister ship, *U-518*, crept into Conception Bay. The U-boat stayed above the waterline but hugged the craggy cliffs on the side of the bay, listening to the sounds of cars travelling on the cliffs above them as it crept closer to its target. The searchlights from the battery illuminated two ships at anchor. The U-boat commander fired at the first, the *Anna T*, but missed. The torpedo slammed into the Scotia Pier, blowing a portion of it to pieces and causing $30,000 damage.[2] The battery immediately responded and while the searchlights swung wildly in an attempt to locate the U-boat it fired again, sinking the *Rose Castle*. Once again the attacking U-boat was able to escape unscathed.

The Canadian government was so concerned about Newfoundland that it created a secret plan to burn St. John's to the ground should it be captured by the Germans. But Newfoundland was not the government's only worry. U-boat activity in the St. Lawrence did not slow and in 1942 was still showing signs of increasing. The Canadian government was busy contending with a growing rumour mill, its angry provinces, and frustrated allies.

On September 9, 1942, an exasperated Canadian government finally closed the St. Lawrence to all but local, coastal traffic. The closure had no discernible effect on North American shipping and was seen as more symbolic than strategic. However, the closure did mean that the ships would no longer have to wait in the dangerous Gulf for other ships to arrive from Montreal and Quebec City before forming a convoy to cross the Atlantic. It also shifted the centre of Canadian shipping away from Quebec and into the Maritime provinces.

Buoyed by their successes in disrupting Atlantic shipping routes, the Germans discovered another use for their U-boats. In May 1942, they landed a spy using the alias of Lieutenant Langbein in the Bay of Fundy, New Brunswick. In November a U-boat deposited German agent Werner von Janowski near the town of New Carlisle, on Chaleur Bay in the Gaspé region of Quebec. Von Janowski roused the suspicions of a local innkeeper's son when he used outdated money and Belgian matches. He was picked up by the Royal Canadian Mounted Police the day after he landed and soon agreed to act as a double agent for the RCMP. Langbein managed to remain in Canada undetected until 1944, but it is unlikely that he was inclined to do much damage as a spy. He and von Janowski had both been tasked with monitoring shipping traffic on the St. Lawrence but that traffic had virtually halted soon after they landed. In fact, RCMP records suggest the Langbein was a friendly man with an encyclopedic memory who had lived in Canada prior to the start of the war and was eager to take advantage of an opportunity to return. According to most contemporary reports, Langbein simply lived off the money provided to him by the German Foreign Office until it ran out and then he turned himself into Canadian authorities.

In September 1943 a U-boat left the village of Kiel, Germany, bound for Canada. Unlike the many other submarines that had gone before it *U-537* was not after North American convoys or cargo. *U-537* carried an interesting cargo of its own, a small group of scientists and technicians. Their mission was to land in Newfoundland and install a weather station nicknamed "Kurt" that could be used by the German High Command for assessing possible invasions of Canada and North America. The weather station was a complex instrument that was able to translate temperatures, wind speed, air pressure, and direction into Morse code and transmit the data every three minutes.

On October 22, *U-537* hovered just off the northern end of Labrador. Despite the danger presented by the numerous air patrols that swept the region, the submarine broke the surface and dropped its anchor. Under cover of one of the area's notorious fogs, the submarine waited at the surface while technicians muscled the 220 pound canisters containing the weather stations components onto rubber boats. The Germans had cleverly marked the canisters with the Canadian Weather Service logo in order to forestall any suspicions should the canisters be discovered. The only problem was that there was no organization known as the Canadian Weather Service in 1943. The German technicians had also brought along American cigarettes and matchbooks to leave at the site and forestall any suspicions should the site be explored by the Canadians. They need not have worried. The remote weather site was never investigated by the Canadians or their allies. The station operated perfectly for a few days, sending out regular signals, and then it abruptly stopped transmitting. It was never used by the Germans.

The existence of the weather stations was a closely held secret known only to a handful of scientists and to the officers of the U-boat who had landed it. The Canadians remained oblivious to the existence of the German weather station until the 1980s when a German historian found a photograph of a weather station that did not fit with the images he had seen of known German weather stations in the arctic. The coast looked much more like that he had seen in Labrador, Canada. He wrote to W.A.B. Douglas, the official historian of the Canadian Armed Forces. Douglas and members of the Canadian Coast Guard made a trip to the suspected location and were able to recover the remnants of the weather station. The historians had also discovered that a second weather station had been dispatched in 1943 but it had been sunk along with the U-boat that carried it in the Atlantic.

During the Second World War, Canada was home to several extensive military prisoner of war installations. One of these prisoner of war camps was in Bowmanville, just outside Toronto, Ontario. Camp 30 was located in a former boy's school and housed some illustrious prisoners including Otto Kretschmer, an infamous U-boat commander who had sunk no less than 42 ships before he was captured in 1941. In October 1943, the commanders of Camp 30 ordered that

Attack on Estevan Point

The east coast was not the only Canadian shoreline under attack during the Second World War. Japanese submarines frequently cruised off the west coast, drifting down from battles in the Aleutian Islands and other locations in the north Pacific. Most British Columbians were blissfully unaware of the danger that lurked just offshore. In the spring of 1942, two incidents occurred that severely challenged the sense that the war was confined to battlefields far from Canada.

On June 19, 1942, a Canadian freighter, the Fort Camosun, *was just rounding the tip of Cape Flattery on the northwestern shore of Washington, when it was torpedoed by the Japanese submarine I-25. Luckily the ship was carrying a load of wood, which allowed it to stay afloat until it reached port. The attack on the* Fort Camosun *was particularly frightening for British Columbia. Canada's Navy was still tiny in the early days of war and the convoy system used to protect ships on the eastern seaboard had not been duplicated on the west coast. The only ships available to protect the west coast of Canada were the Fisherman's Reserve, a motley collection of fishing boats whose owners and crew had offered their services to the Royal Canadian Navy.*

While one Japanese submarine was attacking the Fort Camosun *off the southern tip of Vancouver Island, another was turning its guns on the Estevan Lighthouse on the northern tip of the island. The submarine fired 25 to 30 rounds of 5.5" shells but failed to hit the lighthouse or the nearby village of Hesquiat. No casualties were reported, but the attack marked the first time that enemy shells had struck Canadian soil since the war of 1812.*

In response to the attacks, the Canadian government ordered all lights doused at the outer stations, which proved disastrous for merchant ships attempting to navigate the area. A rudimentary early warning system on the outer islands proved to be only slightly more helpful. Teams of watchers, consisting of a woodsman, a cook, and two telegraph operators, were installed on the remote Queen Charlotte Islands to watch for any sign of a Japanese attack on the Pacific. None came. The next attack was launched in the sky rather than in the sea.

100 German officers, including Kretschmer, be shackled together in retaliation for a recent German order to shoot to kill Allied Commandos.[3] The German officers refused to co-operate and barricaded themselves in the camp mess, armed with iron bars and sticks. Unable to dislodge the POWs, Camp 30 called for reinforcements from another camp. One hundred guards from another camp, armed solely with baseball bats, arrived to help and attempted to storm the mess. The German POWs held them off for three days until an exasperated camp commander finally ordered his men to turn the camp's fire hoses on the mess. The Germans finally emerged and surrendered. The "Battle of Bowmanville" was over.

Additional attempts were made to liberate German POWs in the Maritimes. One U-boat, en route to a hoped for rendezvous with escaped prisoners from POW Camp 70, came under heavy fire from the Canadian Navy when the escape attempt was foiled. The Germans might have thought that the Canadian Navy was underfunded and unprepared, but by 1943 Canada was the third largest naval power in the world and controlled a fleet of no less than 400 ships. The RCN's efforts to expel the German U-boat menace were getting more successful. The Royal Canadian Air Force was becoming equally successful in its efforts to harass the U-boats. Even the Germans acknowledged that their naval efforts were stalling. In late 1943, Grand Admiral Karl Dönitz despaired, "We've lost the Battle of the Atlantic!" The U-boat wolf packs had become flocks of lambs. The St. Lawrence was reopened in April 1944.

The German High Command, faced with the growing threat and a dearth of successes was desperate to recover their star U-boat commander, Otto Kretschmer. An elaborate plan was concocted in which Kretschmer would be removed from Camp 30 via a tunnel. A U-boat would pick him up in New Brunswick. The plan was expected to take nine months to complete. Throughout the summer of 1943 the POWs worked in shifts, digging the tunnel with tin cans. The dirt was removed in bags that were scattered over the rafters in the attic of one of the cabins housing the POWs. By the end of the summer the tunnel, dug 4.5 metres below ground, extended over 90 metres. Unfortunately

Surrender of the German submarine U-889 off Shelburne, Nova Scotia, May 13, 1945.

for the ecstatic would be escapees, the Canadians knew all about their tunnel. When the escape attempt was made only one man managed to get away. He was eventually recaptured in New Brunswick before he was able to meet the expected U-boat.

U-boats remained in Canadian waters until the end of the war. The HMCS *Clayoquot* was sunk near Halifax on Christmas Eve, 1944, and on April 16, 1945,

CANADA UNDER ATTACK

the HMCS *Esquimalt* was sunk near the same spot where the *Clayoquot* had met her end. The U-boat that had taken the *Esquimalt* surrendered to the Royal Canadian Navy one month later and the submarine was recommissioned by the RCN before it was purposely sunk in an elaborate ceremony — in the very spot that it had sunk the *Esquimalt* — several years after the war had ended.

CHAPTER TWELVE:
THE FIRE BALLOONS

The Japanese Attack on Western Canada

The war in Europe and the war in the Pacific had dragged on for over five years, but in the rural Saskatchewan community of Minton it still seemed very far away. On January 12, 1945, the war came crashing down on Saskatchewan. An 11-year-old boy named Tony Frischholz[1] was one of the first to see it. As he walked along a rural road he saw a strange object bouncing down the road in toward him: a huge hydrogen-filled balloon, almost 10 metres wide. Tony did not know it at the time but the balloon also carried a payload of bombs, enough to destroy the entire Frischholz family. The balloon had already travelled several thousand kilometres across the Pacific Ocean and floated over the Rocky Mountains to drop its payload in the Saskatchewan badlands.

Others had also encountered the balloon that day. It did not take 13-year-old Ralph Melle long to figure out what the balloon carried. Melle was wedged between his uncle and his dad as they travelled in his dad's pickup truck on their way into town. The balloon suddenly appeared alongside the road and Melle watched, entranced, as the enormous globe slowly descended into a badlands valley. His father slowed the truck and all three jumped out to take a closer look. Melle unknowingly stepped on one of the incendiary devices. Luckily that bomb failed to go off, but another destroyed a fence when it suddenly exploded. The group noticed that the balloon and its dangerous cargo had strange markings on it, markings that were soon identified as Japanese characters and numbers.

The strange sight that Frischholz and Melle had encountered was a Japanese fire balloon — a *fu-go* — and it was one of nearly 1,000 that landed in Can-

A Japanese incendiary paper balloon that landed off Point Roberts.

ada, the United States, and Mexico between the fall of 1944 and April 1945. Japanese engineers had designed the balloon bombs to take advantage of the continuous jet stream of air that occurs high in the atmosphere, which could be counted on to carry the balloons all the way from Japan to the vulnerable American coastline. Their plan was simple and might have proved devastating, if it had worked.

CANADA UNDER ATTACK

By 1944, the Japanese had suffered several major military defeats, including the Battle of Midway, and desperately needed a way to boost civilian morale, divert allied troops, and create a new battlefront on North American soil. Unfortunately, designs for the first Japanese plane capable of a trans-Pacific bombing were still on the drawing board so an aerial attack seemed out of the question. In the early 1930s, during the Sino-Japanese War, the Japanese military had carried out experiments, using prisoners of war, with balloons designed to carry both biological warfare agents and military personnel behind enemy lines. The experiments had ended with that war but this new war, and Japan's recent defeats in particular, had renewed interest in those experiments. Japanese military officials conferred with meteorologists and decided that a bombing attack carried out with balloons might just work. The Japanese government hoped that the effort would provide them with a respite from bad news, boost civilian morale, and, with any luck, divert allied troops from other battlefields in order to defend the home front. The plan was to launch balloons carrying incendiary devices that would spark large-scale forest fires in the vulnerable and notoriously dry Canadian and American west.

The Japanese military originally designed balloons that were six metres in diameter, able to stay aloft for more than a day, and cover a distance of 3,000 kilometres. But the balloons would have to be launched by submarines lying off the coast of North America — a dangerous prospect, particularly after the defeat at Midway. Faced with those challenges, Japanese engineers designed a much larger balloon — 10 metres in diameter — that could be launched from the islands just off mainland Japan. The balloons themselves were made of laminated panels of paper, shellacked and held together by a potato-based paste. A few were made from panels of silk. They were primarily constructed by Japanese schoolchildren whose school days were frequently shortened in order to accommodate their contribution to the war effort. Few people in Japan, certainly none of the schoolchildren, were aware of the purpose of the balloons. They probably would not have believed it even if they had known. The idea just seemed too fantastical. The reality was much more so.

When fully inflated, the balloons could hold in excess of 6,000 cubic metres of hydrogen.[2] A pressure-release valve detected and released air according to changes in pressure. Hanging 16 metres below the balloon, suspended by ropes that hung like a chandelier, was a device that took measurements and controlled gunpowder charges that in turn released sand from sandbags that surrounded the device. Also on board were magnesium incendiaries, an anti-personnel bomb, an acid block to destroy any remnants of the device, and some magnesium flash powder to ignite whatever hydrogen remained in the balloon after it had touched down. The goal was maximum destruction and they used every piece of the fire balloon to achieve that. Japanese engineers also quickly discovered that if they kept the balloon's payload at less than 170 kilograms it could rise up to eight kilometres high, more than enough for it to ride well out of range of the Allies' radar and aircraft.

The first fire balloon was launched on November 3, 1944. It is unknown if that balloon reached North America, but the first discovery of a fire balloon was made the next day in the Pacific Ocean, 102 kilometres southwest of San Pedro, California, by the United States Navy. In Canada the first word that the Japanese were targeting the Canadian West arrived with a collection of balloon fragments discovered by civilians near Stoney Rapids, Saskatchewan. The Allies were stunned when the first discovery was made. They were completely unaware of the jet stream and it seemed inconceivable that these devices — whose markings clearly identified them as Japanese — could have made the journey from Japan, more than 8,000 kilometres away. Instead, they focused their attention on finding a potential launch site for the fire balloons somewhere in the waters off the North American coastline. Some experts speculated that the balloons had been launched on North American beaches by landing parties from Japanese submarines. Other, wilder, theories suggested they had been launched from German prisoner of war camps or even Japanese-Canadian internment camps.

The only thing the Allies were certain of was that one of the most pressing threats from the balloons was the threat to Canadian and American morale and their potential to boost sagging morale in Japan. Therefore, it was imperative that the Canadian military ensure that no word of the balloon attacks reached the

CANADA UNDER ATTACK

Japanese. The Canadian government also recognized the possibility of mass hysteria if the public learned of the hazards that were sailing across the ocean toward them. They immediately requested that the media refrain from publishing any news of the balloons, a request that the patriotic wartime media quickly agreed to. In an almost unprecedented move, generals from each of the Allied commands in Canada, the United States, and Mexico met with the various media outlets to brief them. Through official channels, the fire balloons would be known only under the code name "paper." The media blackout was so successful that only one news report filtered out to the Japanese.

But while the media blackout served its purpose in minimizing Japanese claims of success and preventing mass hysteria, it also had other, more dangerous, effects. When the Royal Canadian Mounted Police arrived to take custody of a downed balloon north of Delburne, Alberta, in March 1945, they discovered that souvenir hunters had been there first and stripped it of its most critical parts. In another incident that same month a sheepherder was taking his flock to another field when he heard a loud explosion. Later that day he returned to find his cabin completely demolished. A few days later a nearby rancher heard his cattle bawling and found them tangled around what he thought were the remnants of a weather balloon. He tossed the balloon and threw what he assumed to be its recording device in the toolbox of his truck. A few weeks later the annoyed farmer dropped the "recording device" on the desk of the local RCMP officer and let him know what he and the weather service could do with it. The perplexed RCMP officer called a superior, who calmly informed him that the toolbox likely contained a bomb that would level his office. The device was contained and a controlled explosion revealed that the expected bomb was no longer attached to it. Authorities concluded that the payload had actually landed on the sheepherder's cabin.

On May 5, 1945, a minister and his wife took five children from their church on a Sunday picnic in the mountains outside of Lakeside, Oregon. As the children and the minister's wife scurried ahead looking for the perfect picnic spot they stumbled upon a balloon stranded high in a tree. Intrigued, the children tugged on its ropes, hoping to dislodge it. Suddenly, an explosion ripped through the woods. The minister raced toward his wife but it was too late. She and all of the children perished. The public was initially told that they were victims of an unidentified explosive device, but one month later the American military finally officially admitted to the existence of the fire balloons. A few weeks later the grieving minister was finally able to tell his story to the *Seattle Times*. "As I got out of my car to bring the lunch, the others were not far away and called to me they had found something that looked like a balloon," the Reverend recalled, "but just then there was a big explosion. I ran up there — and they were all dead."[3]

While media silence greeted the arrival of the fire balloons in North America, across the Pacific the Japanese were loudly lauding their new weapon. Through the Japanese media they claimed to be wreaking great havoc with the balloons and even claimed to be on the verge of sending manned balloons to invade North America. In a Japanese propaganda program, broadcast in English on February 17, 1945, the Japanese military claimed to have set western North America afire and inflicted 500 casualties with their fire balloons. These broadcasts were sent to North America, Europe, Southeast Asia, and China and all repeated a similar theme: the fire balloon strategy was working. One broadcast even claimed that several million airborne troops would soon land in North America. Although it was doubtful that the fire balloons could carry those kinds of troops, both Canadian and American officials did fear that the balloons might be used like they had been during the Sino-Japanese War experiments, to transport biological warfare agents to North America. Those who studied the balloons believed that such uses were at least theoretically possible, but there is no evidence that they were ever used for that purpose. Squads of 4-H Club members and others were organized to act as decontamination squads, and farmers were told to watch for and report any signs of illness in their livestock. In an effort to aid in locating balloons, some trappers, ranchers, and rural postmasters were also informed of the existence of the fire balloons and asked to remain vigilant and report anything suspicious.

CANADA UNDER ATTACK

The RCMP and the Royal Canadian Air Force joined forces in investigating balloon sightings with an eye to determining their purpose and their source. In one instance, near Minton, Alberta, they tracked a balloon as it repeatedly touched down and rose again. On one touchdown, the balloon dropped a bomb that was discovered and reported by two children. The RCMP and RCAF continued to track the balloon through reported sightings and damaged fences, finally discovering it almost intact in a farmer's field near Minton. It proved to be a valuable find, providing intelligence on the type and size of the explosive and incendiary bombs attached to the balloons. It also provided evidence in the form of the sand from several intact ballast bags discovered with the balloon. Geologists at Canada's National Research Council worked with the United States Geological Survey to analyze the sand and eventually proved that it had been taken from beaches in Japan, stunning Allied military experts with the news that the balloons had indeed sailed all the way from Japan, and allaying public fears that Japanese submarines were lying in wait off Canada's shores.

The researchers were eventually able to pinpoint the origin of the sand to beaches on Honshu, northeast of Tokyo, and the origin of the balloons to three separate sites near those beaches. American fighter jets were scrambled and eventually took out two of the factories. At home, once the Canadian military had discovered the origin of the balloons they were left wondering what to do with them. Most of the time they were too late to do anything — reported sightings were often hours old before they reached the appropriate personnel and the balloons were either already lost or had landed. Planes were scrambled with orders to shoot down the balloons but official records of those sorties are very brief. Apparently, with orders to maintain silence about the balloons in mind, many of the official memos merely record the pilot's altitude and the fact that the pilot shot down "paper."

While the RCAF tackled balloons that were found in the air, other military personnel were dispatched on foot to recover downed balloons. In one instance, a Captain Charles East took his snowshoes into the Saskatchewan bush to locate a balloon that had been reported tangled in a tree. He walked slowly

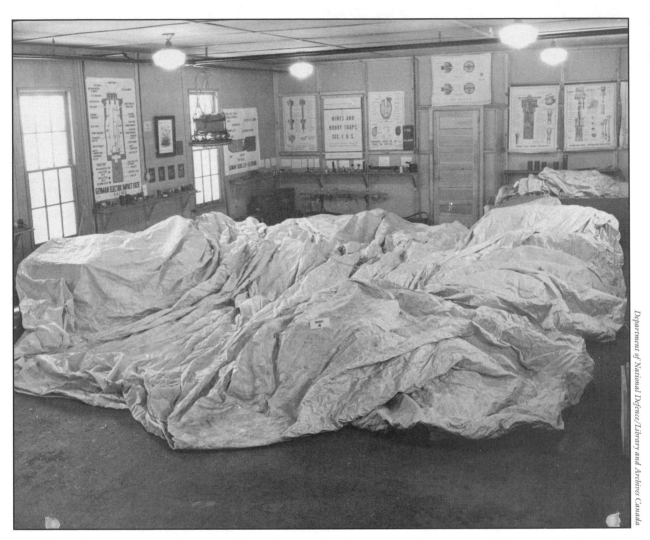

Incendiary balloon partially spread out with the top of balloon in the foreground.

around the tree, binoculars in hand, to try to determine if the bombs dangling from the balloon might still detonate. While he was walking, his snowshoe became caught on something and he tugged to free it. Finally he looked down and saw an object sticking out of the snow. It was an unexploded bomb and he had almost tripped it.

CANADA UNDER ATTACK

Despite the threats posed by unexploded bombs, and Japanese claims to the contrary, the picnickers in Oregon were the only casualties of the Japanese fire balloons. While the balloons may have caused small bush fires, most of the bombs and incendiary devices failed to ignite or cause the devastation they were intended for. Launched during the wet spring and fall months, the balloons did not spark any large-scale fires. On almost every level, the project was an unmitigated failure. Of the over 9,000 fire balloons launched by Japan, less than 1,000 reached their targets in North America. The media blackout ensured that there was no public panic; in fact, the blackout was so successful that few in Canada know of the existence of the balloons even today.

There were several reasons for the failure of the Japanese fire balloon invasion. Clearly the season chosen for the attack played a role. So did the device's design. Historians point out a significant flaw in the ballast dropping mechanism. It was powered by a battery that was contained in a plastic box filled with antifreeze. The antifreeze solution proved to be too weak and the batteries froze as they reached the highest altitude. Many of the balloons were subsequently forced down into the Pacific by the weight of their ballast bags as the battery and the ballast-dropping mechanism failed.

The Canadian public was officially informed of the existence of the fire balloons at the end of May 1945. Although Canadian officials could not have known, the Japanese had actually ended their fire balloon campaign over a month before. The last fire balloon was shot down in British Columbia on April 20, 1945, by an RCAF Kittyhawk, after two children saw it descending through the clouds. But the public would continue to report balloons sailing overhead for many months to come. Most were likely sightings of the planet Venus turned into something more ominous by a nervous public. The RCAF, unwilling to take chances, continued to send out aircraft to pursue these phantom fire balloons sightings, much to the chagrin of its pilots, one of whom lamented in his pilot log, "Three scrambles today. Two of them chasing planets again. Surely someone at control should know sufficient astro-navigation to plot the visible planets in the day time and not scramble 40,000' ceiling mosquitoes thousands of light-years up."[4]

A New Cold War

The latest invasion of Canadian territory is taking place far in the north and the weapons of choice appear to be icebreakers, scientists, and geologists. For centuries the people who vied for control of Canada largely ignored its Arctic regions. But beneath that frozen expanse lies rich, largely undiscovered stores of oil, gas, and minerals. With climate change making these riches more accessible, several countries are challenging Canada's claim to the area. The most serious challenge has come from Russia.

In 2007, two Russian mini-submarines descended four kilometres to the Arctic seabed, where they collected geologic and water samples and left a titanium canister containing a Russian flag on the ocean floor. It was not the first time the Russians had made moves on Arctic lands claimed by Canada. The Russian government had long claimed the North Pole was attached to Russia by an underwater mountain range, but a bid for ownership based on that claim was rejected by the United Nations for lack of evidence. The claim has since been revived and Russian authorities have announced that the Arctic is a critical component of Russia's economic future and that teams of scientists will be sent to the region to find evidence to support Russia's claims.

The Canadian government has responded by reiterating their own claim to the Arctic, increasing the reach of Canadian environmental law over northern waters, and insisting that all ships in the area register with the Canadian Coast Guard. The government has also been vocal in the media and international circles, promoting its Arctic sovereignty.

So far the invasion has been limited to exploration and sabre rattling, but with experts estimating that 10 billion tons of oil and gas reserves that add up to 25 percent of the Earth's available resources, and significant deposits of diamonds, gold, platinum, and other precious metals at stake, this war may eventually heat up. Canada and Russia are not the only combatants. The United States, Norway, and Denmark are also reinforcing their own claims to the region.

Despite the frustration of the pilots forced to track balloons that did not exist, the danger to Canadians did not end once the Japanese suspended their balloon campaign. During the six month campaign the fire balloons managed to cover most of the Canadian west. They landed or were shot down in the Yukon, Northwest Territories, Saskatchewan, Alberta, and British Columbia, which saw the most balloons — over 57 recovered during the six months of the fire balloon invasion. Hundreds of balloons remained undetected in western Canada's woods, fields, and mountains. In fact, one of the last was discovered in British Columbia in the 1990s. Others may still be lying somewhere deep in the Canadian bush.

CHAPTER THIRTEEN:
WAR PLAN RED

By the end of the 19th century, most Canadians were confident that the United States had abandoned the concept of manifest destiny and its acquisitive interest in Canada. Certainly the Americans had provided a lukewarm response to the activities of the Fenians, but they had vindicated themselves in the First World War, coming slowly but decisively down on the side of the Allies and Canada. Relations between the two countries, frequently strained by disagreements over land and alliances, had matured. The longest undefended border in the world was safe. But in 1974 the U.S. government routinely declassified documents. They had done the same thing many times before with little fanfare, but that time a Duke University history professor named Richard A. Preston was busy sorting through a variety of historical documents as research for a book he was writing on Canadian American Relations.[1] In the U.S. Military History Collection, located in Carlisle Barracks, Pennsylvania, he discovered one of those recently declassified documents. It revealed that the U.S. had not given up on plans to invade Canada. Far from it. They had, in fact, prepared an elaborate researched plan that outlined how an invasion of Canada could successfully be carried out.

Stored in a dusty vault, *The Joint Army and Navy War Plan: Red*, had been written in the 1920s, accepted by the United States Secretaries of War and of the Navy in 1930, and updated in 1934 and 1935. The 95-page document, with "SECRET" stamped across its cover, laid out a complex plan in for the invasion of Canada. The invasion plan was part of a war plan known as *War Plan Red*, ostensibly a plan for a pre-emptive strike against Britain via Canada in the event that the two countries went to war. War Plan Red was part of a larger series of war plans drafted between 1918 and 1939 by the U.S. Department of War Planning. Those plans also included War Plan Orange, a plan to invade Japan, and War Plan Green, a plot to invade Mexico.

While it was designed to cover contingency plans for a war with Great Britain, War Plan Red contains very few references to that country. The only theatre of war mentioned in the plan was Canada, referred to as "Crimson." There was also nothing defensive about the plan. The goal of the plan, its authors wrote, was, "ultimately to gain control of Crimson."[2] The earliest draft of the plan, approved by the U.S. cabinet in 1924, went further, suggesting that all territory gained during the operations (that is, all Canadian lands) would be held in perpetuity by the United States. The Government of Canada would be abolished. The capture of Canada was not expected to be easy on the Canadian population. The plan authors expected "consequent suffering to the population and widespread destruction and devastation"[3] in Canada. The United States intended to start the war and even if Canada declared neutrality it was to be invaded and occupied.

The plan contained a detailed analysis of Canada's geography, population, and, most importantly, the country's military strength. It concluded with this stark statement: "Crimson (Canada) cannot successfully defend her territory against the United States (Blue)."[4] In fact, espionage reports from the period on Canada's defensive readiness were often as stinging as they were blunt. Canada acknowledged no known enemies, had failed to maintain a proper air force, and was, therefore, largely unprepared to defend itself.

Halifax was to be the first target. The capture of that port city would logically prevent the arrival of reinforcements from Great Britain and would leave the rest of Canada vulnerable. Several routes were considered, but in the end War Plan Red called for a sea-borne surprise attack from Boston. The attack would have to take place even before war was declared, to maintain the element of surprise and ensure that the city would fall quickly. The next stage of the plan called for the immediate capture of power plants in the Niagara region. Once those were secure the U.S. Army would launch a three-pronged attack. They would take Montreal and Quebec via Vermont, seize the rail lines in Winnipeg from bases in North

Dakota, and then swing up through Michigan and Sault Ste. Marie to take the valuable nickel mines in Sudbury.

In 1935 the plan was altered and the newer version called for an immediate and massive pre-emptive bombing of Vancouver, Quebec, and Montreal, in order to ensure a quick victory over those cities. The amendment further recommended the use of poison gas against Canadians prior to the actual invasion by U.S. troops. Interestingly — and in an echo of the bombing of Nagasaki and Hiroshima — American authorities felt that the tactic was a humanitarian act, as it would end the war more quickly and save both American and Canadian lives in the end. The newer version of the plan also authorized the strategic bombing of the city of Halifax, Nova Scotia, in the event that U.S. troops were unable to defeat and occupy it. While the army invaded by land, the navy would seize control of the Great Lakes and establish blockades of both the Atlantic and Pacific coasts.

In February 1935, the U.S. Congress appropriated $57 million on behalf of the U.S. War Department. The money was to be used to build three air bases along the Canadian-U.S. border that could be used for pre-emptive air strikes on Canadian airfields. The bases were to be disguised as civilian airports and were supposedly a well-guarded secret. Then, in February 1935, Brigadier General F.M. Andrews, Chief of the General Headquarters force, and Brigadier General Charles E. Kilbourne, former of head of the Army War Plans Division, testified in a secret meeting of the Congress Military Committee. The testimony revealed the provision for "camouflaged" air bases on the Canadian border and suggested that the United States "must be prepared to seize nearby French and British Islands in an emergency." The testimony provided by military experts to the committee was explosive and could even be considered slightly hysterical. There are, the experts testified,

> [C]ountless operating bases within a radius of action of this country in the vast number of sheltered water areas that are available deep in Canada … from which pontoon-equipped aircraft could operate at will … There is no necessity for starting with

an observation in order to know what they are going to bomb. They know now what they are going to bomb. They know where every railroad crosses every river. They know where every refinery lies. They know where every power plant is located. They know all about our water supply systems. Their location is most difficult for us to learn, for our own air force to learn. We have to hunt them up. We have to find out where they are before we can attack them. [5]

Interestingly, the U.S. military already knew an extraordinary amount about Canada and its resources. In 1919, they had gathered substantial information on Canada's railroads and highways and a few years later the U.S. Army War College led a study of Canada's airports, harbours, and radio stations. Shortly before Captain George gave his incendiary testimony, a secret mission in the Canadian wilderness had searched for the location of air bases and float planes.

The supposedly secret testimony was mistakenly published with the rest of the committee's proceedings in February 1935. In April 1935, a *New York Times* reporter stumbled on the revelations and revealed them. The article was reprinted in newspapers around the world, and outraged the citizens of numerous countries including Canada, Great Britain, and France. The administration of then-President Franklin D. Roosevelt immediately attempted damage control and the president issued a stinging rebuke of the Military Committee, in which he wrote, "I call your special attention to the fact that this government not only accepts as an accomplished fact the permanent peace conditions cemented by many generations of friendship between the Canadian and American people but expects to live up to, not only the letter, but the spirit of our treaties relating to the permanent disarmament of our 3,000 miles of common boundary."[6]

Despite Roosevelt's assertions, in March 1935 General Douglas MacArthur suggested an additional amendment adding Vancouver to the list of priority targets. The latest amendment even included a list of the best possible roads for the invasion route. For Vancouver that was Route 99.

CANADA UNDER ATTACK

In August 1935 over 35,000 U.S. troops converged on the Canadian border just south of Ottawa for a series of war games. The scenario designed for these war games was a massive invasion of Canada. The war game plan called for the Canadian forces to repel the initial attacks. It then called for an additional 15,000 reinforcements to be brought from Pennsylvania, which was expected to outnumber and outgun the Canadian forces, who would eventually capitulate. The games were considered to be a resounding success by the U.S. military and were one of the largest peacetime manoeuvres in history.

Following the success of the war games, the U.S. military purchased additional lands around Fort Drum and greatly expanded the base. The expansion received a tremendous amount of attention and many Canadians along the border nervously eyed the buildup of troops and weapons to the south. If they had also learned of the existence of extensive plans for the invasion of Canada their reaction would have been much stronger — unless they had also learned that the Canadians had developed their own plan for invading the United States, nine years before War Plan Red was developed.

Defence Scheme No. 1 was the creation of Canada's Director of Military Operations and Intelligence, James Sutherland "Buster" Brown. It was presented to Canadian military strategists in April 1921. Like War Plan Red, Defence Scheme No. 1 was designed as a pre-emptive strike. Also like War Plan Red it was to be launched prior to any official declaration of war. However, Sutherland's scheme was less strategic and based more on the twin premises of surprise and strength, a *levee en masse* as he termed it. "The first thing apparent then in the defence of Canada is that we lack depth," wrote Brown. "Depth can only be gained by Offensive Action."[7]

From bases along the border, thousands of Canadian troops would pour into Washington, Montana, Minnesota, New York, and Maine and overwhelm specific cities in those states. Brown did not expect that his plan would allow the Canadians to conquer America. Instead, his goal was to slow an American attack until Canada's allies could arrive to help. Therefore, the plan also included contingency plans for a retreat in which the Canadian Army would burn bridges and railways to hinder an American pursuit. Brown and several other military men even conducted reconnaissance to support their plan, travelling through a variety of U.S. states dressed in civilian clothing. Brown's plan initially received a considerable amount of support from the Canadian military before being officially abandoned by Canadian authorities a few months before the United States began work on its own invasion plan

In 1939 War Plan Red also faded in importance as the world's attention was captured by the image of the great German Army bearing down on Poland.

NOTES

Chapter One

1. L'abbé Ivanhoe Caron, ed., *Journal de l'expédition de chevalier de Troyes* (Quebec: La Compagnie de L'Eclaireur, 1918).
2. D.W. Prowse, *A History of Newfoundland* (Portugal Cove: Boulder Publications, 2002), 216.
3. Jean Baudoin, *Journal du voyage que j'ay fait avec M. d'Iberville, Capitaine de Frigate de France en l'acadie en l'isle de terre-neuve,* November 10, 1696.
4. John Clapp et al, in a petition sent to William III in 1697 begging for relief and for armed forces to defend the settlers of Newfoundland.
5. Baudoin, November 17, 1686.
6. Baudoin, November 30, 1686.
7. Baudoin, November 30, 1686.
8. Baudoin, November 30, 1686.

Chapter Two

1. Ben Franklin to his brother, John Franklin, Philadelphia, 1745.
2. Estimates vary. Some put the cost as high as $200 million dollars, others report that it cost barely half of the 30 million livre estimate. £30 million is, however, the most commonly quoted figure and can be found in such sources such as William Wood's *The Great Fortress (A Chronicle of Louisbourg 1720–1760)*, and Robert Emmet Wall in the *New England Chronicle*. Interestingly, the reconstruction of barely one-fifth of the fortress, begun in the 1960s, cost

over $25 million Canadian, and took 20 years to complete.

3. Quoted in William Wood, *The Great Fortress (A Chronicle of Louisbourg 1720 –1760)* (Toronto: The Hunter-Rose Company, 1920), 34.
4. Lettre d'un Habitant de Louisbourg, 36.
5. Wood, 30.
6. Lettre d'un Habitant de Louisbourg, 15.
7. Letter of Monsiery DuChambon to the Minister at Rochefort, September 2, 1745.
8. Louis Effingham DeForest, ed., *Louisbourg Journals 1745* (New York: Heritage Books, 1998).
9. Lettre d'un Habitant de Louisbourg, 35.
10. An anonymous soldier in the Fourth Massachusetts Regiment quoted in Louis Effingham De Forest, ed., *Louisbourg Journals 1745* (New York: Heritage Books, 1998), 27.
11. Quoted in Henry S. Burrage, *Maine at Louisbourg* (Augusta, ME, Burleigh & Flynt, 1910).
12. Burrage, 51.
13. Eric Krause, Carol Corbin, and William O'Shea, ed., *Aspects of Louisbourg: Essays on the History of an Eighteenth Century French Community in North America* (Sydney, NS: University College of Cape Breton Press, 1995), 128.
14. Wood, 76.
15. From a composite prepared from a number of primary sources in Robert Emmet Wall, Jr. "Louisbourg 1745," *New England Quarterly*, Vol. 37, No. 1, March 1964, 66.
16. Quoted in John Stewart McLennan, *Louisbourg from Its Foundation to Its Fall, 1713–1758* (Detroit: The University of Michigan, 1918), 237.
17. Quoted in Wood, 121.
18. In the 1960s the Canadian government launched a project to rebuild Louisbourg. Today the massive fort stands guard at the mouth of the St. Lawrence once more, but now it is manned by Parks Canada rather than the French Army.

Chapter Three

1. Wolfe in a letter to Amherst, August 8, 1758.
2. Beckles Willson, *The Life and Letters of James Wolfe* (London: W. Heinemann, 1909), 417.
3. Wolfe in a letter to his mother, November 13, 1756.
4. Sir Arthur John Doughty, ed., *The Journal of Captain John Knox, Volume 1* (Santa Barbara, CA: Greenwood Press, 1968), 93.
5. James Wolfe quoted in Sir Leicester Harmsworth, *The Northcliffe Collection* (Ottawa: F.A. Acland, printer to the King's Most Excellent Majesty, 1926), 111.
6. Montcalm in a letter to Marshal de Belle Isle, Montreal, April 12, 1759.
7. This was the same Captain Cook who would later earn fame as an adventurer and explorer in the South Pacific.
8. William R. Nester, *First Global War: Britain, France and the Fate of North America 1756–1775* (Westport, CT: Praeger Publishers, 2000), 132.
9. Estimates of Montcalm's troop strength vary according to the source. Montcalm himself estimated that he had just over 13,000 but that number might not include some of the militia or thousands of Native troops who had allied themselves with the French.
10. Wolfe quoted in George M. Wrong, *The Conquest of New France: A Chronicle of the Colonial Wars* (Whitefish, MT: Kessinger Publishing, 2003), 90.
11. Wolfe's First Manifesto, Beckles Willson, *The Life and Letters of James Wolfe* (London: W. Heinemann, 1909), 439.
12. Jean-Félix Richér, *Journal du Sèige de Québec en 1759* (Quebec: Société de Historique de Québec), 59.
13. Marie de la Visitation, "Narrative of the Doings During the Seige of Quebec, and the Conquest of Canada," Thomas Thorner, ed., *A Few Acres of Snow: Documents in Pre-Confederation History* (Toronto: University of Toronto Press, 2003), 99.

14. *Ibid*, 100.
15. Wolfe quoted in *The Life and Letters of James Wolfe*, 453.
16. Wolfe in a letter to his mother, Banks of the St. Lawrence, August 31, 1759.
17. Montcalm to Artillery Officer and Secretary Montbelliard.

Chapter Four

1. Paul David Nelson, *General Sir Guy Carleton, Lord Dorchester: Soldier-Statesman of Early British Canada* (Cranbury, NJ: Associated University Presses, 2000), 93.
2. Michael P. Gabriel, *Major General Richard Montgomery: The Making of an American Hero* (Cranbury, NJ: Associated University Presses, 2002), 142.
3. Carleton to Lord Dartmouth, Quebec, November 20, 1775.
4. Carleton quoted in Nelson, 72.
5. George Washington to the Continental Congress, from his camp at Cambridge, September 21, 1775.
6. Sir James Carmichael Smyth, *Precis of the Wars in Canada* (New York: C. Roworth, 1826), 79.
7. Arnold to George Washington, Chaudiere Pond, October 22, 1775.
8. George Morison's journal, November 1775.
9. William Renwick Riddell, *Benjamin Franklin's Mission to Canada and the Causes of Its Failure* (Toronto: University of Toronto Press, 1923), 130.
10. *Ibid.*, 133.
11. *Ibid.*, 133.
12. *Ibid.*, 134.
13. Mark Zuehlke, *Canadian Military Atlas* (Vancouver: Douglas & McIntyre, Ltd., 2001), 58.

Chapter Five

1. The Nootka are also known as the Mowachahts or Muchalaht First Nation. They originated in the Friendly Cove area of Nootka Sound. In historical texts they are frequently referred to as the Nootka Natives.
2. Gilbert Malcolm Sproat, *Scenes and Studies of Savage Life* (London: Smith, Elder and Co., 1868), 12.
3. Warren L. Cook, *Flood Tide of Empire: Spain and the Pacific Northwest, 1543–1819* (New Haven, CT: Yale University Press, 1973), 58.

Chapter Six

1. Isaac Brock letter to Captain James Brock, Kingston, 1811.
2. Ferdinand Brock Tupper Esq., ed., *The Life and Correspondence of Sir Isaac Brock, K.B.* (London: Simpkin, Marshall & Co., 1845), 172–73.
3. Isaac Brock letter to Captain James Brock, July 1812.
4. Walter Nursey, *The Story of Isaac Brock: Hero, Defender and Saviour of Upper Canada, 1818* (Toronto: W. Briggs, 1909), 97.
5. Mary Beacock Fryer, *Bold, Brave, and Born to Lead: Major General Isaac Brock and the Canadas* (Toronto: Dundurn Press, 2004), 72.
6. Nursey, 101.
7. John Boileau, *Half-Hearted Enemies: Nova Scotia, New England and the War of 1812* (Toronto: Formac Publishing Company, Ltd., 2007).

Chapter Seven

1. Louis Joseph Papineau in a speech to the Six Counties, Saint-Charles, October 31, 1837.

2. Dr. Wolfred Nelson in a speech on October 23, 1837.

3. George Nelson's Journal, Nelson Family Papers, Toronto Public Library.

4. George Bell, *Rough Notes of an Old Soldier* (London: Day and Son, Ltd., 1867), 51.

5. Amédée Papineau, *Journal d'un Fils de la Liberté Réfugié aux États-Unis par suite de L'insurrection Canadienne, en 1837*, Vol. II (Montreal: Éditions L'Étincelle, 1978), 46–47.

6. Bell, 55.

7. Jean-Joseph Girouard to M. Morin, April 28, 1838, quoted in John Hare, ed., *Les Patriotes, 1830–1838* (Montreal: Libération, 1971), 144.

8. The Seventh Report from the Select Committee of the House of Assembly of Upper Canada on grievances, 6.

9. Daniel Webster to Lord Ashburton on the Case of the *Caroline*, Department of State, June 27, 1842. This has become an internationally accepted precedent and was used most recently by the United States to justify its invasion of Iraq.

10. Lord Durham's Report, 1839, 51.

Chapter Eight

1. *The New Yorker*, Saturday March 23, 1839, 12.

2. From an account told by Eleazer Packard to the *Whig and Courier*, Bangor, Maine, reported in the *Daily Courier*, Hartford, Connecticut, February 20, 1839.

Chapter Nine

1. Thomas Newbiggen, "Fenian Raids: Invasions of British-Ruled Canada," Historynet, 3–8 of printed materials; *www.historynet.com/fenian-raids-invasions-of-british-ruled-canada.htm*.

2. *Ibid.*, 3.

3. John O'Neill, *Official Report of General John O'Neill, President of the Fenian Brotherhood, on the Attempt to Invade Canada* (New York: John F. Foster, 1870).
4. Estimates vary widely depending upon the source.

Chapter Ten

1. Henry Landau, *The Enemy Within: The Inside Story of German Sabotage in America* (New York: G.P. Putnam's Sons, 1937), 19.
2. Kaltschmidt quoted in *The Enemy Within*, 45.
3. David Ricardo Williams, *Call in Pinkerton's: American Detectives at Work for Canada* (Toronto: Dundurn Press, 1998), 182.
4. Williams, 182.

Chapter Eleven

1. Steve Neary, *Enemy on Our Doorstep: The German Attacks on Bell Island* (Toronto: Jesperson Press, 1994), 12.
2. *Ibid.*, 56.
3. The Commando Order was a secret directive issued by Adolph Hitler on October 18, 1942. It stated that all Allied commandos operating in either Europe or Africa should be killed immediately. This applied even if the commandos were in uniform or if they tried to surrender. Any soldier who refused to carry out this directive would face a court martial.

Chapter Twelve

1. CBC Radio Archives, *World Report*, "Japan Bombs Saskatchewan," broadcast

February 7, 2005.

2. Brendan Coyle, *War on Our Doorstep: The Unknown Campaign on North America's West Coast* (Surrey, BC: Heritage House Publishing, 2002), 218.

3. "Saw Wife and Five Children Killed by Jap Balloon Bomb," the *Seattle Times*, June 1, 1945, 1.

4. Major Mathias Joost, "Western Air Command and the Japanese Balloon Campaign," *Canadian Military Journal*, Summer 2005, 65.

Chapter Thirteen

1. R. A. Preston, *The Defence of the Undefended Border: Planning for War in North America, 1867–1939* (Montreal: McGill-Queen s University Press, 1977).

2. *Ibid.*, 226.

3. War Plan Red, 1935, 6.

4. Major Charles H. Jones, Infantry, Chairman and Lieutenant Colonel H.W. Crawford, Engineers, *Supplement No. 3 to Report of Committee No. 8; Subject: Critical Areas of Canada and Approaches Hereto; Prepared by Committee No. 3*, 51.

5. Captain H.L. George, *February 11–13, 1935, Hearings of the Committee on Military Affairs, House of Representatives, on Air Defense Bases*, 51.

6. Franklin D. Roosevelt as quoted in "U.S. Disavows Airport Yarn," the *Globe and Mail*, Wednesday May 1, 1935, 2.

7. *Defence Scheme No. 1*, April 12, 1921, Chapter One, Section 3.

SELECTED BIBLIOGRAPHY

Baudoin, Jean. *Journal du voyage que j'ai fait avec M. d'Iberville, Capitaine de Frigate de France en l'acadie en l'isle de terre-neuve*. November 10, 1696.

Bell, George. *Rough Notes by an Old Soldier*. London: Day and Son, Ltd., 1867.

Boileau, John. *Half-Hearted Enemies: Nova Scotia, New England and the War of 1812*. Toronto: Formac Lorimer Books, 2007.

Brock, Sir Isaac. *The Life and Correspondence of Major-General Sir Isaac Brock, K.B.* Ferdinand Brock Tupper Esq., ed. London: Simpkin, Marshall & Co., 1845.

Burrage, Henry S. *Maine at Louisbourg*. Maine, MA: Augusta, Burleigh & Flynt, 1910.

Caron, Ivanhoe L'abbé, ed. *Journal de l'expédition du chevalier de Troyes*. Quebec: La Compagnie de L'Eclaireur, 1918.

Cook, Warren L. *Floodtide of Empire: Spain and the Pacific Northwest, 1543–1819*. New Haven, CT: Yale University Press, 1973.

Effingham de Forest, Louis, ed. *The Journals of Louisbourg*. New York: Heritage Books, 2008.

Fryer, Mary Beacock. *Bold, Brave and Born to Lead: Major General Isaac Brock and The Canadas*. Toronto: Dundurn Press, 2004.

Gabriel, Michael P. *Major General Richard Montgomery: The Making of an American Hero*. Cranbury, NJ: Associated University Presses, 2002.

Hare, John, ed. *Les Patriotes, 1830–1839*. Montreal: Libération, 1971.

Karr, William. *Explorers, Soldiers and Statesmen*. New York: Ayer Publishing, 1938.

Knox, Captain John. *The Journal of Captain John Knox, Volume 1*. Sir Arthur

John Doughty, ed. Santa Barbara: Greenwood Press, 1968.

Krause, Eric, Carol Corbin, and William O'Shea, Eds. *Aspects of Louisbourg: Essays on the History of an Eighteenth Century French Community in North America*. Cape Breton: Cape Breton University Press, 1995.

Landau, Henry. *The Enemy Within: The Inside Story of German Sabotage in America*. New York: G.P. Putnam's Sons, 1937.

Lesperance, John. *The Bastonnaise: Tale of the American Invasions of Canada, 1775–1776*. Toronto: Belford Brothers, 1877.

Macleod, Peter D. *Northern Armageddon: The Battle of the Plains of Abraham*. Vancouver: Douglas and Macintyre, 1998.

McLennan, John Stewart. *Louisbourg from Its Foundation to Its Fall 1713–1758*. Detroit: University of Michigan, 1918.

Nelson, Paul David. *General Sir Guy Carleton, Lord Dorchester: Soldier-Statesman of Early British Canada*. Fairleigh Dickinson University Press, 2000.

Nester, William R. *First Global War: 1756–1775: Britain, France and the Fate of North America*. Westport: Greenwood Publishing Group, 2000.

Nursey, Walter. *The Story of Isaac Brock*. Harvard University: W. Briggs, 1909.

Papineau, Amédée. *Journal d'un Fils de la Liberté Réfugié aux États-Unis par suite de L'insurrection Canadienne, en 1837*, Vol. II. Montreal: Éditions L'Étincelle, 1978.

Preston, R. A. *The Defence of the Undefended Border: Planning for War in North America, 1867–1939*. Montreal: McGill-Queen's University Press, 1977.

Prowse, D.W. *A History of Newfoundland: From the English, Colonial and Foreign Records*. Portugal Cove, NL: Boulder Publications, 2002.

Riddell, William Renwick. *Benjamin Franklin and Canada: Benjamin Franklin's Mission to Canada and the Causes of its Failure*. Toronto: University of Toronto Press, 1923.

Smyth, Sir James Carmichael. *Precis of the Wars in Canada: From 1755 to the Treaty of Ghent in 1814*. New York: C. Roworth, 1826.

Sparks, Jared. *The Diplomatic Correspondence of the American Revolution*. Boston: Nathan Hale, 1830.

Sproat, Gilbert Malcolm. *Scenes and Studies of Savage Life*. London: Smith, Edler, 1868.

Thomas, Morley K. *Metmen in Wartime: Meteorology in Canada*. Toronto: ECW Press, 2001.

Tucker, Glenn. *Tecumseh: A Vision of Glory*. New York: Cosimo Inc., 2005.

Williams, David Ricardo. *Call in Pinkerton's: America's Detectives at Work for Canada*. Toronto: Dundurn Press, 1998.

Willson, Beckles. *The Life and Letters of James Wolfe*. London: W. Heinemann, 1909.

Wood, William. *The Great Fortress: A Chronicle of Louisbourg, 1720–1760*. Toronto: Hunter, Rose & Company, 1920.

Wrong, George M. *The Conquest of New France: A Chronicle of the Colonial Wars*. New York: Kessinger Publishing, 2003.

INDEX

MORE GREAT DUNDURN TITLES
FOR YOUNG PEOPLE

True Stories of Rescue and Survival
Canada's Unknown Heroes
Carolyn Matthews
978-1-55002-851-5
$19.99

A crab boat off Newfoundland catches fire, and a rescue is undertaken by helicopter. A child goes missing in a New Brunswick forest, and a desperate hunt is mounted. A climber falls on a British Columbia mountain, and a helicopter rescue is attempted. A civilian chopper crashes in Nunavut, and a search-and-rescue team braves a savage snowstorm to find survivors.

True Stories of Rescue and Survival features the above true stories and many more from across the country, past and present. Its heroes are to be found in the RCMP, city police forces, the Canadian military, and among all the rescue workers and specialists of the Canadian Coast Guard.

Sidebars spotlight the equipment search-and-rescue teams use, how search dogs are trained, how long-line rescues work, how navy divers are making a difference in the deserts of Afghanistan, and much more.

Day of the Flying Fox
The True Story of World War II Pilot Charley Fox
Steve Pitt
978-1-55002-808-9
$19.99

Canadian Second World War pilot Charley Fox, now in his late eighties, has had a thrilling life, especially on the day in July 1944 in France when he spotted a black staff car, the kind usually employed to drive high-ranking Third Reich dignitaries. Already noted for his skill in dive-bombing and strafing the enemy, Fox went in to attack the automobile. As it turned out, the car contained famed German General Erwin Rommel, the Desert Fox, and Charley succeeded in wounding him.

Author Steve Pitt focuses on this seminal event in Charley Fox's life and in the war, but he also provides fascinating aspects of the period, including profiles of noted ace pilots Buzz Beurling and Billy Bishop, Jr., and Great Escape architect Walter Floody, as well as sidebars about Hurricanes, Spitfires, and Messerschmitts.

Men of Steel
Canadian Paratroopers in Normandy, 1944
Colonel Bernd Horn
978-1-55488-708-8
$19.99

Take a trip back in time to the chaos and destruction of the greatest invasion in military history, viewed through the lens of Canadian paratroopers. *Men of Steel* is the exciting story of some of Canada's toughest and most daring soldiers in the Second World War.

In the dead of night, on June 5, 1944, hundreds of elite Canadian paratroopers hurled themselves from aircraft behind enemy lines. That daring act set the stage for the eventual success of the Allied invasion fleet. From aircraft formations striking out from England on a turbulent flight across the English Channel to the tumultuous drop over Occupied Europe and deadly close combat in the Normandy countryside, *Men of Steel* is a detailed account of Canadian paratroopers and their instrumental role in D-Day.

Available at your favourite bookseller.

 DUNDURN PRESS
www.dundurn.com

What did you think of this book?
Visit www.dundurn.com for reviews, videos, updates, and more!

Marquis Book Printing Inc.

Québec, Canada
2010